# BORN TO DIE IN MEDELLIN

D0713283

## ALONSO SALAZAR

**Translated by Nick Caistor**
**Introduction by Colin Harding**

First published as *No Nacimos Pa' Semilla*, 1990 by CINEP in Colombia.
© CINEP
Published in UK by Latin America Bureau (Research and Action) Ltd,
1 Amwell St, London EC1R 1UL

A CIP catalogue record for this book is available from the British Library

ISBN 0 906156 66 1 PBK
ISBN 0 906156 67 X HBK

Translator: Nick Caistor
© Introduction: Colin Harding
Editor: Duncan Green
Cover design: Andy Dark
Printed by Russell Press, Nottingham, NG7 3HN
Trade distribution in UK by Central Books, 99 Wallis Road, London E9 5LN
Distribution in North America by Monthly Review Press, 122 West 27th
Street, New York, NY 10001

Printed on environmentally friendly paper.

# Contents

# COLOMBIA

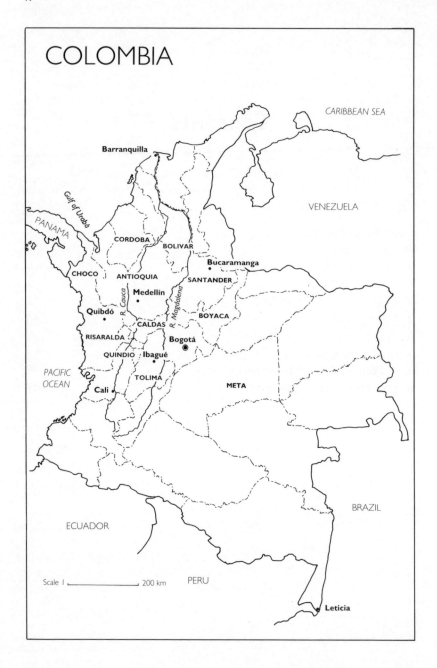

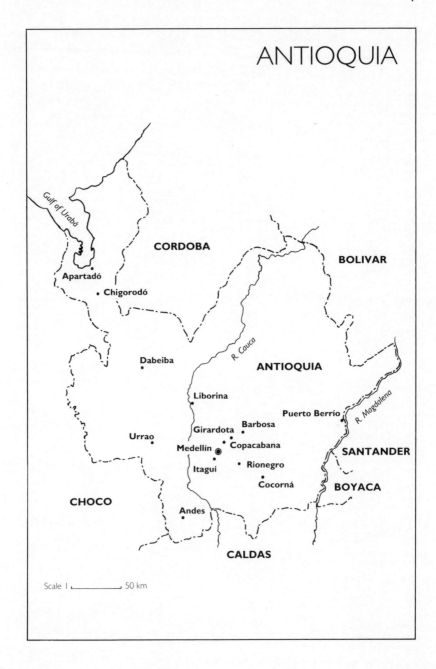

# ANTIOQUIA

Gulf of Urabá

CORDOBA

BOLIVAR

Apartadó

Chigorodó

R. Cauca

Dabeiba

ANTIOQUIA

Liborina

Puerto Berrío

R. Magdalena

Barbosa

Girardota

Urrao

Medellín

Copacabana

SANTANDER

Itaguí

Rionegro

CHOCO

Cocorná

BOYACA

Andes

CALDAS

Scale 1 ⌐————⌐ 50 km

# Author's Preface

Violence is part of everyday life in Medellín. We are living in a city at war. A war involving many powers and fought by young people. They are the ones who kill and die. They enact a script written by others that has its origins in the tragedy which continues to characterise the history of Colombia.

Ours is a war in which it is useless to talk of good fighting evil. The real challenge is to find a way out of this labyrinth in which so many bullets, fired from all sides with a plethora of arguments, are constantly killing us.

Statistics do not lie, but neither do they tell the whole truth about what is happening in our city, in our daily lives, what is happening to us as we live and walk in our streets, our way of relating to our neighbours or passers-by. Medellín is a fabulous place, most of us who live here still say. It's a living hell, others reply, especially outsiders. Medellín is a hotbed of life and death, it is the most extreme expression of the crisis the whole of Colombia is experiencing.

We live in a city where there are lots of people killed, but few who admit defeat. Our efforts, like those of many others, must be to strengthen life and hope. It is a task for which there are more than enough bullets and never enough words.

This book offers a voice to some of the protagonists of the violence. The stories are based on a series of interviews carried out in 1989 and at the start of 1990. We have selected what seemed the most representative interviews out of all those carried out during our research. We have attempted to preserve the style and language of the original accounts, although we have occasionally reorganised them for the sake of coherence and clarity. The names, places and some of the circumstances have been changed for obvious reasons.

In the final chapter we offer some points for consideration that should be seen in the light of what are as yet only provisional studies of the phenomenon.

This study was made possible in the first place by support from the *Instituto Popular de Capacitación* (Popular Training Institute) and was completed under the auspices of the Corporación Región.

I should like to thank all those who have helped me in many different ways during the course of writing this book. Special thanks go to Jorge Ignacio Sánchez, to Camilo Borrero and to Laura Restrepo, for all the encouragement and time they have given me.

Alonso Salazar
Corporación Región

# Introduction

'Medellín, City of Eternal Spring. Enter our competition and win two weeks in Honeymoon City!' The mellifluous tones of the announcer on Radio Ondas del Amazonas make it sound deliciously tempting, particularly if you are sweating it out down in the jungle city of Leticia in the rainy season.

On the other hand: 'The most violent city on New Year's Eve and New Year's Day was Medellín....where 40 people died violently, the police said. Thirty-three were shot or knifed to death and the rest died in accidents at home or on the roads.' (Reuter)

Or try this one: 'Attackers with machine guns shot dead seven young men early Friday in front of a cemetery in the city of Medellín, police said. The victims, between the ages of 20 and 30, were standing on a street corner in front of a local cemetery when the assailants arrived in two vehicles and blocked off several roads.' (AP)

The contrasting images underline both the complexity and the bewildering rate of change in Colombia's second city, the capital of Antioquia department, population 2.5 million. Besides enjoying an agreeable climate and idyllic setting in the mountain-ringed Aburrá valley, Medellín is a long-established manufacturing capital, the Manchester of Colombia, with textile, brewing, chemical and other industries. It's hard to imagine English honeymooners heading for Manchester, but there you are.

The city is also the murder capital of the world, a centre of violence in a country notorious for its apparently casual attitude to life and death. Murder is the greatest cause of death among young males in this home to teenage gangs of *sicarios* (hired killers) and their paymasters, the infamous Medellín cartel. Even now, when all the top cocaine barons are either dead or behind bars, the drug business is thriving and the murder rate continues to grow. What makes this extraordinary place tick?

Perhaps some clues lie in the history of the city and its region, and in the character of its people. The energy and entrepreneurial spirit of the *paisas*, as people from Antioquia are known, are a byword in Colombia, and are often regarded as unique in a country noted for its attachment to tradition and formality. Although originally founded in 1661, probably by Spanish Jews, until the early 19th century Medellín and the rest of Antioquia province remained a remote backwater known only for its gold mines. Then population increase and the lack of other opportunities triggered an explosion of pioneering enterprise.

Thousands of *antioqueños* set off south to bring the wild, mountainous hinterland, which later became Caldas and Tolima departments, into cultivation. At first the frontier families lived by subsistence agriculture, slashing and burning the undergrowth to carve out small farms. In the second half of the 19th century, the emergence of coffee as an export crop for the growing markets of the northern hemisphere gave renewed impetus to *antioqueño* colonisation.

Elsewhere in Colombia, coffee estates were usually large, and belonged to a handful of rich coffee barons. In Antioquia, however, the crop was grown on small family farms. This provided the economic foundation for the subsequent image, or myth, of the sturdy, hard-working *paisa* individualist. In the words of one writer, Antioquia and the colonisation area to the south became 'a democratic society of small proprietors in a continent dominated by great estates. It was different, outside the established, traditional framework of Latin

American societies, and this separateness set free an impressive accumulation of energy for the opening up of land, communications and markets.' It wasn't quite like the winning of the Wild West, but near enough to make country people in this region among the most prosperous in Colombia by the latter years of the 19th century. In 1893 the opening of the Antioquia railway from Medellín down to the Magdalena valley gave the products of the hinterland river and rail routes to the coast and the wider world. The result was a boom in coffee exports that made Colombia the world's leading producer of mild (arabica) coffees until the 1930s.

Coffee gave the expanding rural population of Antioquia and its southern neighbours — the region known as Viejo Caldas, which has since been broken up into the small departments of Caldas, Risaralda and Quindío — a relatively comfortable standard of living, and provided the capital and business experience necessary for launching Medellín into the industrial era in the early years of this century.

Antioquia also has a long mining tradition, stretching back to colonial times, when black women divers were used to extract alluvial gold from the rivers. Mining produced the region's first merchants and financiers and, along with the coffee trade, provided a ready-made pool of business talent and experience when the first big textile mill opened in Medellín in 1906. Within a few years the city was full of cotton factories, attracting migrants from all over the countryside. Many of the great family names of Colombian finance and industry — Echavarría, Ospina, Restrepo — came from the Medellín textile business. By the end of the First World War the city was well established as Colombia's industrial capital, employing some 6,000 textile workers.

In the 1950s the textile industry went into decline, buffeted by foreign competition, but other industries soon took their place, spawning a large working class which suffered the effects of cyclical unemployment and instability long before the cocaine business began to emerge in the region during the early 1970s.

## La Violencia

Before that came the period of Colombian history known simply as *La Violencia*. From the mid 1940s to the late 1950s, as many as 200,000 Colombians — maybe more — died in an orgy of political violence that scarred most of the country and particularly affected Antioquia. Some of it was old-fashioned sectarian killing in which supporters of Colombia's two traditional parties, the Liberals and the Conservatives, attacked each others' villages and butchered as many of the other side as they could lay hands on.

*La Violencia* was largely a rural phenomenon, at least in the early years, but it was never purely sectarian. Much of the violence had social and economic as much as political causes, particularly in Antioquia and Viejo Caldas. In these regions, small family farms had been continually subdivided by inheritance and sale, leaving a large floating population of landless migrant coffee pickers known as *golondrinas* (swallows). Much of the killing in Antioquia involved attempts to force farmers from their land or to steal the coffee crop on its way to market. Hundreds of thousands of gunmen, known as *pájaros* (birds), in the pay of large landowners and businessmen, created havoc in the countryside and forced thousands of terrified peasant farmers to seek refuge in the towns. Places such as Ibagué in Tolima, where the violence was at its most ferocious, grew from a small market town to a city of more than a quarter of a million people in a few years. There is a whole genre of Colombian folksongs about this period, full of nostalgia for the peaceful farms and villages of an idealised past, which came to an abrupt and brutal end with the arrival of the gunmen in the *vereda* (hamlet).

The life histories recounted in this book show a variant on this theme of migration to the towns to escape violence. Many rural *antioqueños* drifted down to the tropical frontier of Urabá, on the Caribbean coast. Urabá had been opened up for banana plantations from the 1930s, but still had plenty of land available for peasant farmers to clear with machetes. The insecurity of this way of life springs from the pages of *Born to Die in Medellín*. Since then, migration from the countryside has turned Colombia into a country of big cities — Barranquilla, Cali, Bucaramanga as well as Medellín and the capital, Bogotá, and it is hardly surprising that violence has migrated to the towns as rural Colombia has slipped into history.

Medellín, the capital of Antioquia, boasts a large university, an active artistic and cultural life and one of the country's great newspapers, the conservative *El Colombiano*. The other, darker side is a large pool of unemployed, poorly educated young people in the *comunas* (poor neighbourhoods). Without any obvious prospects for a legal job, and often with a family background of random violence, they were just what the incipient drug barons needed to develop their business. The appearance of the Medellín cartel in the mid 1970s coincided with a sharp recession in the traditional *paisa* economy. Crime became the only game in town.

As *Born to Die in Medellín* makes clear, the gangs predated the drugs. The shantytown suburbs overlooking the prosperous heart of the city filled with groups of street-corner toughs. Some were recruited and trained in the 1970s and 1980s by Colombia's many guerrilla groups, such as the 19 April Movement (M-19) mentioned in the text. When the army turned the heat on, the guerrillas were forced to abandon the cities, leaving their former apprentices to move on to more lucrative outlets for their newly-acquired skills. Hence the appearance of youth gangs of muggers and hold-up artists until, as in Los Angeles or New York, the drug scene became the thing to get into. In 1980 the Death to Kidnappers (*Muerte a Secuestradores*, MAS) organisation appeared in the wake of the kidnapping of a member of the Ochoa family, one of the cartel kingpins. From then on the level of drug-related killings spiralled.

The Medellín cartel leaders can be seen as genuine products of the local culture, people of mainly humble origin who showed remarkable imagination and self-confidence in building a successful business empire out of nothing. The cartel's best known figure, Pablo Escobar, came from a lower middle-class family in Envigado, near Medellín, and graduated from petty crime to the big time via work as a hit-man for criminal gangs.

Like other *nouveaux riches* the world over, the most successful cocaine *capos* went in for conspicuous consumption (unlike the traditionally puritanical *paisa*). They built themselves sumptuous palaces and bestowed public works, such as sports stadiums, on their home neighbourhoods. In the process, many became Robin Hood-like heroes to the neighbourhood kids. Escobar, for example, built his own safari park in the Magdalena valley, complete with zebras, elephants and kangaroos, acquired a collection of vintage cars and became a substantial landowner with great, heavily guarded estates dotted about the countryside. If the snooty Medellín establishment wouldn't accept them as members, (while for many years turning a blind eye to their illegal activities), men like Escobar and Gonzalo Rodríguez Gacha were capable of going ahead and building their own, rival elite.

## Guns for Hire

Such people had the money and the motive to hire *sicarios* to do their dirty work, and found a ready pool of talent in the poor neighbourhoods in the north-east of the city, where a motor bike and a gun became passports to easy money and the consumer lifestyle rammed down young throats by the media. Inevitably, their activities spawned another form of violence: the 'vigilante' squads who took it upon themselves to 'clean up' the neighbourhoods overrun with young thugs. They are still at large, cleaning up after the drug barons have departed the scene, but the petty dealers and gangs are still around, looking for a new racket — 190 gangs were identified in Medellín in 1990. These days the 'self defence' units are often run by left-wing political groups, giving a whole new dimension to the neighbourhoods.

Into this maelstrom step organisations such as Corporación Región, which commissioned this book, first published in Colombia in 1990 as *No Nacimos pa' Semilla*. Development corporations and vigilantes alike have helped organise street festivals, carnivals and other events to try to overcome people's fear of leaving their homes and to lay claim again to a street life that had been destroyed by the nightly gunfire and the dawn harvest of corpses.

Research institutes, business organisations and the government itself all have an interest in trying to understand what has happened to Medellín. Sociologists such as Alonso Salazar have emphasised social mobility as the root of the city's gang culture. Violence has become a way for young men to make their way in a society that has closed its doors to them. He attaches great importance to the ceaseless consumerist bombardment to which they are subjected by the media, which constitutes a permanent invitation to take by whatever means necessary. He also stresses that violence is an everyday occurrence, of which the political and drug-related killings are only a relatively minor part. Gang culture involves the very young. At the bottom of the hierarchy of violence are the *pelados*, the kids, who are already learning their craft at the ages of 12 or 13, secure in the knowledge that few crimes are punished.

Does this desperate scene leave any room for optimism about the future? Surprisingly, people like Salazar think that it does. The *sicarios* and their victims are *paisas*, after all, inheritors of a great entrepreneurial tradition. But the inevitability of violent death must be ended, the feeling that the kids are *desechables*, disposable, born only to be thrown away after use. Local and national governments are now pouring in money to rehabilitation schemes for gang members, setting up training courses, creating jobs — anything to give them a better occupation than killing for a living.

It is worth remembering, as Salazar notes, that the violence of Medellín is not the violence of decline. The city is booming economically, even as the murder rate spirals. But as long as so many are excluded from the benefits of *paisa* prosperity there will always be plenty of young men ready to resort to the gun to get their share.

Colin Harding
April 1992

# 1

# The Lords of Creation

Silhouetted against the full moon, the shape of a headless cat strung up by its paws. Its blood has been collected in a bowl on the floor. Only a few drops continue to fall. As each one hits the bowl it makes tiny ripples, which grow until the whole surface seems full of tossing waves. Waves that shake to the noise of heavy rock being played at full blast. The cat's head is in the corner, its luminous green eyes staring sightlessly. Fifteen people are taking part in the silent ritual. The city is spread below them.

Warm blood is mixed with wine in a glass. The blood of a cat that climbs walls, leaps nonchalantly from fence to fence, walks on the silent pads of its paws across rooftops, vanishes effortlessly into the shadows of night. Cat's blood, full of the urge to pounce unerringly on its prey. Blood that conjures up strange energies, that speeds the brain.

Antonio recalls in a jumble of images the moment of his own initiation into one of the teenage gangs in a neighbourhood on the hills of north-east Medellín. In his feverish dreams as he fights for life, he sees himself on the streets again. Strange shapes appear in the sea of city lights. They raise the cup to seal their pact. There is no need for words, they all know what they are committing themselves to, what the laws are, the rewards and the punishment. From now on they will be all for one and one for all, they will be as one. They'll be the lords of creation.

But now Antonio is in the San Rafael Ward of the Saint Vincent de Paul hospital. A military ward, full of the wounded and the dying, the victims of an unequal war waged day and night along undefined fronts on the streets of Medellín. One Tuesday, three months earlier, Antonio was blasted with a shotgun as he boarded a bus in his neighbourhood. The shot perforated his stomach, leaving him hovering between life and death. Although only twenty, Antonio has often faced death, but has never felt it so close to him. He knows, even though he won't admit it, that he's not going to make it. He has a skinny body, a face drained of colour, dark eyes sunk in huge sockets. He begins to tell me his life story in a calm voice, searching inside himself, as if taking stock for reasons of his own.

## Antonio

When I was a kid I used to get a bit of money using a home-made pistol. Then Lunar and Papucho — they're both dead now — let me have proper guns, so I started to steal and kill for real. You get violent because there are a lot of guys who want to tell you what to do, to take you over, just because you're a kid. You've got to keep your wits about you, to spread your own wings. That's what I did, and off I flew; anybody who got in my way paid for it.

I learned that lesson from my family. From the old woman, who's tough as nails. She's with me whatever I do. She might not look much, but she's always on my side. The only regret I have in quitting this earth is leaving her on her own. To know she might be all alone in her old age. She's fought hard all her life, and she doesn't deserve that.

My old man died about 14 years ago. He was a hard case too, and taught me a lot, but he was always at the bottle, and left us in the lurch. That was why I had to fend for myself, to help my ma and my brothers and sisters. That's how I started in a gang — but also because it was something inside me, I was born with this violent streak.

Lunar, the leader of the gang, was only a teenager but he was tough all right. He'd been in the business for years already. He lived in Bello for a while and knew the people from Los Monjes. He learned a lot from them, so when he came to live here he started up his own gang. He had a birthmark or *lunar* on his cheek, that's how he got the nickname. It was thanks to him and Papucho, the other leader, that I learned how to do things properly.

I'll never forget the first time I had to kill someone. I had already shot a few people, but I'd never seen death close up. It was in Copacabana, a small place near Medellín. We were breaking into a farmhouse one morning when the watchman suddenly appeared out of nowhere. I was behind a wall, he ran in front of me, I looked up and was so startled I emptied my revolver into him. He was stone dead. That was tough, I won't lie, it was tough for me to take. For two weeks I couldn't eat a thing because I saw his face even in my food... but after that it got easy. You learn to kill without it disturbing your sleep.

Now it's me who's the gang leader. Papucho was killed by the guys up on the hill there. They set a trap for him and he fell for it. They asked him to do a job for them, then shot him to pieces. A friend of his was behind it, who'd sold out. Lunar made me second-in-command because we understood each other almost without speaking — we didn't need words.

Lunar didn't last much longer; he was never one to back down from a fight, never a chicken. He really enjoyed life; he always said we were all playing extra time anyway. And he was enjoying himself when he died: he was at a dance about three blocks down the hill when they shot him three times in the back. He was on his own because he reckoned there were no skunks down there. The kid who shot him died almost before he could blink. We tracked him down that same night, and sent him on his trip to the stars.

After Lunar's death another wise guy thought he'd take over the gang. I had to get tough and show him who was boss. For being such a smart ass now he's pushing up the dirt as well. It's me who gives the orders round here, I say what we do and don't do. There were about fifty of us to begin with, but a lot of them have been killed or put inside, and others have grassed. There's only twenty of us real hard cases left. They're all teenagers, between 15 and 18. I'm the oldest. A lot get killed or caught, but more always want to join, to get some action.

Whenever anyone wants to join I ask around: 'Who is this kid? Can I trust him?' Then I decide if he can join or not. They're all kids who see things as they are; they know they won't get anywhere by working or studying, but if they join us they'll have ready money. They join because they want to, not because we force them. We don't tell anybody they have to. Not all of them are really poor, some do it for their families, others because they want to live in style.

Before we finally choose someone we give him a test: to take something somewhere, to carry guns and to keep them hidden. Then finally we give them a job to do. If the kid shows he can do it, then he's one of us. But if he ever grasses on us, if he shoots his mouth off, if he gets out of line, then he's dead meat. Everyone understands that. Then again, we support each other all we can; 'If you haven't got something and I have, take it, friend — as a gift, not a loan'. We also help if someone's in trouble. We look after each other, but nobody can double-cross us.

We take good care of our guns, because they're hard to come by. The last kid I shot died because of that.

'Antonio, help me out will you brother? Lend me a gun for a job I have to do,' he said to me.

'I'll let you have this .38, but be sure you give it back tomorrow; you know the rules.'

I lent it to him because the kid had always been straight with us, but this time he wasn't. So I went to talk to him, and he came up with a really strange excuse. He said the law had taken it from him. I gave him another two days, and when he didn't show up I passed the death sentence. He knew he was a marked man, so he didn't make any attempt to hide. It was easy for me.

The thing is, it's hard to find guns. You either have to shoot a guy to get his, or buy them, and a good weapon costs. We nearly always buy them from the police, and they sell us the ammo too. I've also bought grenades from a retired army guy. We've had T-55s, 32-shot mini-Uzis, 9mm Ingrands, but we usually use sawn-off shotguns, pistols and revolvers. We're all good shots.

We practise late at night, two, three in the morning, in some woods over at Rionegro. We set up a line of bottles and fire at them. I smash the lot. You have to keep a steady hand when you're on a job, you only have one chance to kill someone, you can't afford to miss. You only have a few seconds so you have to know what you're doing: if the dummy doesn't die, you could. You have to know how to handle your weapon, to shoot straight, and how to make your get-away. We learn a lot from films. We get videos of people like Chuck Norris, Black Cobra, Commando, or Stallone, and watch how they handle their weapons, how they cover each other, how they get away. We watch the films and discuss tactics.

We learn to ride motor bikes on the hills round here. They're all souped up, really quick. Most of them are stolen; we buy papers for them for 20,000 pesos[1] down at the traffic police. Our territory is from the bus terminal down to the school. People who don't mess with us have no problems, but anyone who tries to muscle in either gets out or dies. We help the people in our neighbourhood, they come to us and say: 'we've got nothing to eat', so we help them and keep them happy. And when we've done a job that pays well, we make sure they get some. We look after them so that they're on our side. Whenever someone tries to move in on our

1.  £1 = 545 pesos (1990).

territory, I personally go and kneecap them as a warning they should never come back.

Lots of kids in the neighbourhood want to be in a gang. All I tell them is if that's what they want to do they have to be serious about it, but I don't force them to join. Most of them start by stealing cars, then they save up to buy a shotgun, which is the cheapest weapon around. We give them cartridges so they can get started.

I reckon I've killed 13 people. That's 13 I've killed personally, I don't count those we've shot when we're out as a gang. If I die now, I'll die happy. Killing is our business really, we do other jobs, but mostly we're hired to kill people.

People from all sorts of places contract us: from Bellavista jail, from El Poblado, from Itagüí. People who don't want to show their faces, and take you on to get rid of their problem for them. I try to work out whether our client means business, if he can pay us. We charge according to who we have to hit: if he's important, we charge more. We're putting our lives, our freedom, our guns on the line. If we have to leave the city to deal with some big shot, our price is anything up to three million. Here in Medellín the lowest we go is half a million.

We don't care who we have to give it to, we know it has to be done, that's all there is to it. Whoever it may be: I have no allegiances. I'll drive the bike and gun anyone down myself, no problem. Sometimes we don't even know who it is we have to kill. You hear later who the hit was, from the news on the radio. It's all the same to us, we've done our job, that's all.

Whenever I have to kill someone, all I think is: too bad for him he crossed my path. If their back is towards me, I call out, so I can make sure I've got the right guy, and when he turns round, I give it to him. I don't worry about it, I don't worry about running into the law, or that things will go wrong, nothing like that. I only hope I don't kill a woman or a child in a shoot-out. If I'm going to kill, there has to be a reason for it.

Once we went out to a small town to deal with a local councillor. We don't usually know who is giving us the contract, but in this case it was more or less direct contact, and we realised that the guy who wanted him dead was the leader of a political party. We kept well away from him after that, because you can be the ones who end up paying. They can easily have you rubbed out as well to get rid of witnesses. We made a million on that job.

The week before, we went to the town to see the lie of the land. We were shown the client, we took a look at where the police were, worked out how to get out afterwards. On the Saturday, I went back with a girlfriend. She was carrying the weapon — a submachine gun — in her bag. We took a room in the best hotel, pretending we were a honeymoon couple. We took our time checking out the town, making sure nothing could go wrong.

On the Sunday, two of the gang stole a car in Medellín, and kept the owner in a room in Guayaquil until the job was done. One of them drove to the town and parked where we'd agreed, right on time. The councillor always liked to have a coffee in a corner bar after his meetings. My girlfriend showed up with the gun around two in the afternoon. I took it and waited for the action. Waiting like that really gets you down. You get real nervous. I've found a trick which always helps me: I get a bullet, take out the lead, and pour the gunpowder into a hot black coffee. I drink the lot, and that steadies my nerves.

At ten to six I left the hotel and sat waiting in the bar. It was a hot evening, and there were a lot of people on the street. I saw our car arrive and park a few metres away. The target came in a couple of minutes later. On the dot as promised.

It was beginning to get dark, which is always useful. I took another good look round to make sure there was nothing unusual going on, then paid for my drink. When the waiter was giving me my change, I pulled out the submachine gun and started firing. Everybody hit the floor. When something like that happens in a small town, they all stay well out of it, no one is expecting it. I went over and put a final bullet in him, because some of these guys are really tough and you have to make sure of your money. It was all over in seconds. While I had been firing, they had started the car, so I walked to it as calm as could be, and got in. We made sure we didn't drive too fast out of town. We made as if we were going out on the main highway, but then headed off down a side road. We drove for about a quarter of an hour, then left the car by the roadside. We walked for an hour, until we came to a safe house on a farm owned by a friend of the politician who had hired us. We caught a bus back to Medellín about five o'clock the next morning. They sent the gun back to us a few days later. Everything had been well planned and worked like clockwork.

That night we had a huge party. We'd already had the pay-off, so as the saying goes: 'the dead to their graves, the living to the dance'. It was like Christmas. We bought a pig, crates of beer and liquor, set up a sound system in the street, and gave it all we'd got 'til morning.

☆ ☆ ☆ ☆ ☆

The bus struggles up the hill, along narrow twisting streets full of people and shops. From this main road you have to walk another two blocks up a narrow alley-way, then climb a gully before you reach the Montoya family's house. The roof is made of corrugated iron and cardboard; the walls are not plastered, just painted with a blue wash. Red geraniums flower outside. The house is three tiny rooms. Posters of movie stars and rock musicians cover the walls. Lost in one corner under a layer of cobwebs is a small picture of the Virgin of El Carmen. A horseshoe and a piece of aloe vera hang over the front door to bring good luck.

Doña Azucena, Antonio's mother, is a small, thin woman. Her face shows the marks of all she has been through in her life. Two children, aged four and six, whom she had by her second husband, cling to her legs. She works in a cafe in the centre of Medellín. A few years ago, when she still had legs worth showing off, she worked in the Porteño bar in Guayaquil. The kind of bar where men go to drink liquor and pick up women. Doña Azucena takes some photos out of an old album which show her in high heels, a mini skirt, and wearing bright scarlet lipstick. She would never dream of showing them to her children. It was in that bar, to the sound of music from Olimpo Cárdenas and Julio Jaramillo, that her second husband fell in love with her. A much older man, she lived with him for four years until one weekend, she never knew why, he walked out and didn't come back. She didn't miss him, because her older children had never got on with him, and because she herself had lost all her affection for him.

## Doña Azucena

In the bar there's a big picture of a man hanging from a branch. A tiger is trying to climb the tree, there's a rattlesnake in the tree-top, and under the branch is a pool full of crocodiles. I used to look at that picture and think my life was exactly like that. Wherever I've been, I've lost out.

I can remember it like it was yesterday. I was at a rural school in Liborina, a beautiful part of the country. It was May, the month of the Holy Virgin, and we were preparing to celebrate. Our teacher, who was called Petronilla, asked me to pick some roses for the altar, and said I should make sure to cut all the thorns off. I went down a path below the school where there were some lovely rose bushes. I picked them and sat down to snip the thorns off. Then I went back to the school and gave them to the teacher. She took them, but a splinter got caught in her finger, so suddenly she drew back her hand and slapped me across the face. Without even thinking about it, I slashed at her with the knife, the one I'd used to cut the roses. She was badly wounded, but they managed to save her life. That was the end of school for me.

I've always had a quick temper, I've never let anyone put anything over on me. That's how my family was, that's how my children are. I was born in Urrao, but we had to leave there when I was still little because of the political violence. My father, whose name was Antonio too, was a die-hard Liberal, every weekend he'd go into town, get drunk, and start shouting 'Up with the Liberals!' for everyone to hear. As soon as the violence started, we began to get death threats.

Once my father and his brothers had to take on a bunch of Conservative thugs who were terrorising the area. We knew they'd come up after us. So the men borrowed some shotguns and took up their positions on a bit of a hill just below the house. When they saw the Conservatives arrive, they fired at them and they ran off.

That same evening Don Aquileo, a neighbour who was a Conservative too, but who got on well with us, came up to see us. He told us that down in town everyone was saying they'd get together and come up and finish us off. There'd already been other tremendous massacres in the countryside, so we decided to get out that same night and go to Liborina, where we had family. Later some Liberal guerrillas got organised in Urrao, led by Captain Franco. But that was after we left. We had a dreadful time there, I can remember passing lots of mutilated bodies by the roadsides, those are things you never forget.

A few years later, I was a teenager by then, we moved on to Chigorodó, in Urabá, because they said the land was fertile there. We began to clear a farm in the jungle, about two hours from the nearest town. That was where my mother María died. The climate killed her. The weather was impossible. Up there the heat is hellish, and it can rain the whole day long. It was a struggle to clear the jungle, but eventually we were able to plant bananas and maize.

The good times didn't last long. We'd just begun to harvest our crops, when the violence began there too. Not between

Conservatives and Liberals, but just between people for no reason at all. There was a store where we all used to go at weekends to talk and drink. But soon people began to fight with machetes. The men got drunk and killed each other without ever knowing why, or rather, at the slightest excuse.

My brothers have always been difficult, they've fought with almost everyone. But above all they got into trouble with a family called García, who came from Dabeiba. There were about ten of them, all dangerous men. It was when they started threatening us that we decided to sell up and come to Medellín.

We settled in the Barrio Popular. We built a place up on this hill, just when people had started moving in. Soon everywhere was full of shacks. People who had lost their land in the country because of the violence, and had come to the city to escape.

I can remember the day when Don Polo was out laying the floor for his place. He'd come from Andes with his family. The police on horseback turned up, and wanted to take him away. We all used to help each other, to protect ourselves, so I went out and started to shout at them.

'You can't take him if you haven't got an arrest warrant.'

'You're not the law, you bitch, we are, and we know what we're doing,' one of them shouted back, pointing his rifle at me.

I was really angry by then, and I thought well, if I'm going to die then so be it, may God forgive me all my sins but this injustice shouldn't be allowed to happen. Other people began pouring out of their houses. Then a police car arrived. We were still arguing, and one of the police hit me with the butt of his rifle.

'Come on, it's you we're going to arrest for causing an obstruction,' he said, pushing me into the car.

I began to kick out, and my neighbours all closed round the car, saying: 'You've no right to take Doña Azucena.'

'Drive off,' the captain told his driver.

'Which way? D'you want me to kill all these people?'

They all crowded closer and closer round the car, and finally pulled me out. The other policemen on horseback were shouting insults all the time. Then a young fellow hit one of them with a stick, and they all fired at him. The rest of us ran off. They picked up his body and left. They took him to the hospital, but he died. Things like that happened all the time, the police would come up to destroy our houses, but we'd all stand firm. A lot of lives were lost. That's why we've never liked the law, it seems they're always out to get the poor.

It was around that time that I married Diego Montoya. He was a young man who had just moved to Medellín from Puerto Berrío. I went with him against my family's wishes; they didn't like him because he was black. We went to live with one of his sisters over in Santa Cruz. For a few years it was good, he looked after me and remembered all the little details - everything was fine. We had five children, almost one after the other: Claudia, Diego, Antonio, Orlando, and Nelly.

But gradually Diego went downhill. He became a tremendous drinker and would give me almost nothing for the kids, so I had to go and find work, first of all in houses over in Laureles, then in a bar in Guayaquil. One day when I came back from work I found my eldest daughter Claudia with her leg all bloody. Diego's sister's eldest son had sliced her with a saw because she had picked up something he was working with. I took my belt off, went to find the boy, and gave him a good thrashing. His mother tried to defend him, so I started on her too. When Diego came back later that night, I told him what had happened. His sister went whining to him, and told him he should teach me a lesson.

'He's not going to teach me any lesson, you do it if you want to,' I told her.

'But he's your husband,' she replied.

'That he may be, but if I have to show him what's what, I will.'

Diego got really angry and left. By the time he returned I was in bed, reading a magazine by candlelight.

'I'm leaving, thanks for everything. All your things are on the table,' I told him.

I'd put his revolver and some money he'd given me on the table by the bed. He didn't say a word, but got into bed. At about five in the morning, he got up again. He stood there for a minute staring at me, then went over to our daughter's bed, stroked her hair, gave her a kiss, and began to cry.

'Wake up sweetheart, wake up so we can talk about it,' he said to me, shaking me gently by the shoulder.

'There's nothing for us to talk about. I've already given you back all your things, what more do I owe you?'

'Can't you wait 'til Saturday so I can sort things out?'

'When did you ever sort things out? All you do is make one promise after another, then spend every cent you earn on whores or booze.'

'Just wait, in the next few days I'm expecting a big note, I promise I'll hand it over to you,' he begged me, and my heart softened.

'OK, let's see; if you love your children and want to stay with them, then buy us somewhere to live, that's the only condition. I'll give you all day today to think about it, if you don't come up with something by tonight, I'm off.'

He didn't come back to sleep that night, but the next day, Saturday, he arrived very early. He took me and the children to look at a plot of land in the Barrio Popular. We did the deal there and then, and the following week had already built a place. We've been living in this gully ever since.

This is where I brought up my children. Diego died 14 years ago, a few months after he had an accident that crippled him. While he was at home sick he told people's fortunes for them. He knew a lot. Just by looking at the palm of someone's hand he could tell what was wrong, what their illness was, if they had been smoking too much dope, if a woman had the evil eye on them. Then he'd give them a cure or take the spell off them. He learned from his father, who practised these things down in Puerto Berrío. I asked him to teach me, but he always said: 'You're too black-hearted, if you learned this, you'd use it to harm people.'

It's true that in some ways I can be hard. I wouldn't harm a soul, but if anyone crosses me, they're for it. That's what I've always taught my children, that they've got to make people respect them. They've got it in their blood, they were born as rebellious as me. My eldest worked for a while in the building trade, but then he fell in with some friends and began to go wrong. At first they dealt in marijuana, then they started with robberies. At the moment he's doing three years in Acacías, Meta, for assault.

Ever since he was little, Antonio's been the wildest of the lot. The same thing happened to him at school as me, although I've never told them my story. In his third year at primary school they had a teacher who used to punish them terribly, so one day Antonio and a friend waited for him outside the school and stabbed him with a knife. Since then, Antonio's been on the streets.

It was Diego, his older brother, who got him started in crime. Antonio was only eleven when he was sent to a remand home, in Floresta. He'd had a fight with a neighbour's boy, Doña Blanca's son, a kid's quarrel. But then Alberto, her older son, threatened to give him a hiding. I spoke to them and said that if anyone was going to give him a hiding it would be me. In return they insulted me, and that drove my kids wild. Without my knowing it, Diego gave Antonio a gun.

'If you let that Alberto lay a finger on you, I'll give you another hiding myself. You have to show you're a Montoya,' Diego told him.

One day soon after, I was making lunch when I heard some shots and a terrific row outside. I ran out and saw Alberto lying on the pavement. Antonio had shot him five times. Fortunately he didn't die, but since then it's been war between our two families. Two of them have died, and my sons have been wounded several times.

After Antonio got out of the remand home he studied plumbing and electrics at the San José school. But that didn't last long, he was soon back on the streets. A few days later I saw him with a couple of boys who were a good bit older than him, Papucho and Lunar, both of them dead now. They were the ones who sealed his fate. People began to be afraid of them, grassed on them to the police, and they came looking for them.

All I can say is that he's been a good son to me. I've had to work in bars all these years to earn enough to keep my family. It's hard for a woman on her own. Antonio is the one who's helped me the most. He's never drunk a lot, and whenever he's done a job he always brings something back for the house.

I've been with him through thick and thin. Whenever he's inside I always go and visit him. I've often had to struggle with the police, but I've made sure they respect me as a woman. I've made a vow to the Fallen Christ of Girardota to make sure my boy gets well quickly. That's what I want, I want him to get well and go and find the coward who shot him, things can't stay like this. None of my family is going to feel safe with that fellow around.

Antonio knew they wanted to kill him, that's why he left home. That Tuesday, he came up here in the morning and was chatting with the girls, playing with the dog. I went down to the main street to buy things for lunch. As I was coming back I saw two of the Capucho gang on the corner. That scared me, but I walked past them calmly, as if I hadn't even seen them.

'Antonio, get away from here, they're out to get you,' I told him when I reached home.

'Don't worry, ma, the day I die I'll have my bags packed and ready, but today isn't the day,' he said laughing, lying back on the bed.

In the afternoon he went round to his girlfriend Claudia's house next door. He was still joking about, listening to music as if nothing was wrong. At six I saw the others again, they were at the bottom of the gully. They had their hands in their pockets, and were staring up our way. The worst of it was that Antonio didn't have any protection. I went and found him and told him what was going on.

'It looks bad out there, I think you should find some way to get away.'

'Cool it, ma, I'll be off in a minute. Go round to Gitano's place and tell him to bring a couple of guns up here, that there's going to be some action.'

I sneaked out the back way and went to find Gitano.

'Doña Azucena, he's not back from town, and anyway he hasn't got any guns either,' they told me.

When I told Antonio that Gitano wasn't around, he looked worried, but pretended everything was all right.

'I'm going over the wall at the back here,' he said. 'You two go out the front and act normal, while I get away.'

We went out and sat on the front porch to chat. The Capucho boys were still down at the bottom of the gully, so I relaxed a bit. But then 15 minutes later I got a call from the hospital.

'We have your boy Antonio Montoya here, he's in a bad way.'

In the three months since then I've been down there every afternoon between two and five, when you can visit them. Every week the hospital is full of wounded kids, they come and go, new ones take the place of those who get better, but Antonio is still there. I don't know how all this is going to end.

The priest went to give him confession yesterday, I've no idea what Antonio told him about his life. When the priest came out he greeted me very formally. 'Don't worry, he has repented and is at peace with God,' he told me. And that did bring me peace of mind. Even though I'm not much of a believer it's always better to know you're at peace with God.

☆ ☆ ☆ ☆ ☆

## Antonio

I'd like to be out on the streets of my neighbourhood again, that's my territory. I love walking down them. I've always got my wits about me of course, my eyes wide open and my gun in my pocket, because I've got as many enemies as friends. You never know where you might get shot from. A lot of people are after me, I've got a lot of admirers in other gangs. The law is also on my tail. If I get out of here, I'm going to be real careful.

There've always been gangs in our neighbourhood: the Nachos, the Montañeros, Loco Uribe's gang, the Calvos... and as the song says: 'this bed ain't big enough for everyone'. You have to be on the look-out, if you're not careful one of the other gangs muscles in and people start leaving you. You have to make sure of your territory, that's the main thing. The biggest war we ever had was with the Nachos, who were hired killers like us. When they first showed up we did nothing, but then they started throwing their weight around, upsetting people. Until one day Martín, one of our gang, told them where to get off, and they shot him. That same night we went up to their place and taught them a lesson. Six of us went up there in groups of two: we met up on the street corner where they hung out, and took them completely by surprise. We shot two of them. They thought they were such tough guys they never even imagined anyone would come for them.

A few days later they came for us. We were waiting for them. I put a handkerchief over my face, put on a baseball cap, and went out with my submachine gun. Others from the gang were covering me, watching what would happen.

'We want peace, not war,' one of the Nachos shouted.

'We don't want peace, what we want is war,' Lunar shouted back, and fired off a volley into the air.

Of course they didn't really want peace, what they were trying to do was to see all our faces so they could pick us off.

In the end they retreated back up the gully. 'Get them to start making your coffins,' they shouted from up top.

From then on it was war. They would come down into the gully, we'd go and raid them, both sides would try to ambush each other... it was a real shootin' war that left a lot of people dead.

The Nachos went to pieces after the police got their leader in a raid. Even I have to admit that the guy was a real man: he and this other guy were fighting it out with the pigs for hours. They say that when Nacho had only one bullet left he shut himself in the bathroom of the house they were holed up in and shot himself in the head. After that his gang was nothing, they had no stomach for a fight. A few days later the law arrested about twenty of them, and now they're all in Bellavista for a good long while.

The gang wars have been tough: whole families have been wiped out in vendettas. What happens is if one of the gang or one of your relatives gets killed, you go out and get the bastard who did it, or one of his family; but we never touch women. If you don't react, they walk all over you.

We also fight the police, but it's easier with them. They're shit scared when they come up here, and we know our own territory. Of course they've caught me twice, and I ended up in Bellavista as well.

The first time was the hardest. I'd been holed up in a house in a nearby neighbourhood. About midnight I woke up to hear them knocking the door down.

'Open up, this is the police,' they shouted.

I tried to escape out the back, but the place was surrounded. Before I could do a thing, the police were everywhere. They put me into the patrol car without even letting me get dressed, and took me off to the F-2 headquarters. All they found in the house were three guns we had stashed there.

At the station they put me in a tub with water up to my neck. They left me there all night freezing my balls off, and ran electric current through me too. They kept asking me about the others in the gang, who the leaders were, but I didn't say a word.

'Think you're a real tough guy, don't you, you fairy,' they shouted, kicking me as hard as they could in the stomach.

I didn't think I was tough at all, but to grass on people is the lowest you can go. They asked me about enemies of mine, but I didn't even give them away, although I knew where they hung out. It's like Cruz Medina sings in the tango: 'Don't anyone ask who wounded me so, you're wasting your time, you'll never know. Let me die here in peace, and don't be surprised at that, when a man is a man, he won't squeal like a rat'.

I was sent to Bellavista prison for illegal possession of firearms. I didn't have a record, and they couldn't get anything out of me, so they got mad. They even tried to get people from the neighbourhood to testify against me, but nobody would. There may be people who hate your guts, but they know that if they start blabbing, they're signing their own death warrants. Either you get them once you're out, or one of the gang does it for you.

I was three months in the slammer. That was only about long enough to get over the beating the pigs had given me. I met several of the gang in the jail. I was lucky that the boss man on our block was an old guy I'd done a job for, who liked me. If you end up in Bellavista with no one to look after you, you're done for. You get kicked from block to block until you end up in the worst hole, where they steal everything you've got, even your sex.

That's why I was lucky, because I had someone to look out for me. Of course I met up with a few of my old enemies too, some of the Nachos and others. But the worst was a guy called Pepe, whose brother I had shot. I told the boss man about him, and he said: 'Tell him to get out of here, and if he cuts up rough about it, send him to the funeral parlour.'

I sent the message to Pepe, and a few days later he changed blocks. Whatever the boss man says goes. Nobody in there can do anything without his permission.

Once I got into a fight. I had some air-cushion Nike running shoes, the ones that cost 20,000 pesos. Two guys came up to me: 'Listen, sweetheart, get those shoes off, they've been sold,' one of them said, a switchblade in his hand.

'You listen. Tell whoever bought them to come and take them off, I'm too tired,' I said, pulling out a metal bar I had hidden in my jacket.

Three of my gang appeared out of nowhere, and we set on them. I ended up stabbing one right in the heart. He died on the way to the infirmary. The other one got away. One of us was wounded too, but nothing serious. In Bellavista they don't even bother to make any enquiries, they know no one will say a word. Anyone who's been hit gets his own back if he can, if not, he chokes on it.

I paid my way out of Bellavista. There are people who act as go-betweens with the judges. My case was easy, because it wasn't a serious charge and nobody came forward to accuse me of anything else. I paid around 250,000 pesos. Or rather, some associates of the gang who'd just done a job paid it for me.

After that I went back to my patch, to my normal life. Half the time I'm happy, the other half I'm worked up. When I haven't got anything to do, I get up late, it's almost dark by the time I hit the streets. I hang around the street corners listening to rock music with the gang or I go to a bar with my girl to listen to love songs or country music.

My girl is called Claudia. I know I can trust her, she knows what I do, and backs me up, but she doesn't want to get involved at all. She works in a dress factory and comes home early every day. She's got expensive tastes: she likes new clothes, jewels, all the fancy stuff, and I give her everything she wants. At the weekend either we go out to bars in Bello, or dance salsa, or go down into Manrique to listen to some smoochy music. She's a good-looker, but what I most like about her is that she's serious. Because there's a lot of girls who make your eyes pop, but most of them are just good for a quick lay, a one night stand. Sometimes we like to party at the houses we hide up in, and we get girls in. Fabulous women, but they're only out for what they can get from you. The only real girlfriend I've had is Claudia.

☆ ☆ ☆ ☆ ☆

Things have got very difficult. This gang's appeared called the Capuchos, they're killing people all over the place. It was them who shot me. I knew they were after me, that's why I split from home. But then I got it into my head to go up and say hello to the old woman and Claudia. I thought everything was quiet because the police were snooping around the neighbourhood a lot at the time. I didn't want any trouble, so I went up there without a weapon. Ma soon told me that they were out looking for me. I wasn't worried, I knew they wouldn't dare come up to the house. It's in a narrow gully, so long as you're under cover you can take on anyone.

I was waiting for some of the gang to arrive with the guns so we could get rid of those guys. By the time night fell and they hadn't arrived, I realised things were getting serious. So I climbed out of the back of the house and made for the road up top. I walked about a block, and saw a bus coming down, so I waved it to stop. Just as I was getting on, I saw a kid about two metres from me with a shotgun. Then I felt this heat spreading all through my body, and that was the last I knew. I was out for four days before I came round. What got me most was that a lot of people in the neighbourhood knew what was going on but didn't warn me. The Capuchos had every exit staked. I guess it's everyone's turn sometime, and that day it was mine.

What I wish is that they had killed me there and then, without time for me to let out a sigh or feel any pain, or even to say 'they've got me'. I'd have preferred that to this feeling that my body and my mind are being torn apart. Having to stare death in the face all day long, grinning and beckoning at me, but not daring to come any closer. Better to die straight off, so you don't get to see how all your so-called friends abandon you. In here you realise that people are only with you in the good times. As Don Olimpo sings: 'When you're on top of the world, you can have friends galore, but when fate trips you up, you'll see it's all lies, they won't want you any more'. I don't care about dying, we were all born to die. But I want to die quickly, without all this pain and loneliness.

Last night Antonio had his final dream. He dreamt he was up again on the flat roof of the house in the gully where he'd been happiest, blowing his mind with all his gang to the music of drums and electric guitars.

☆ ☆ ☆ ☆ ☆

## Antonio

The city at night is fabulous, it's all light and darkness. I feel just like one of those dots, lost in a sea of light. That's what we are, a tiny light, or maybe a patch of darkness. In the end, we're all or nothing. We can do great things, but we're all mortal. Look closely at the yellow lights, and they turn into all colours, they spread upwards until they make a rainbow in the night. Then they're like a huge cascade of white water that is falling and falling into a deep, invisible well. Then the water gushes out again, this time like a giant flame, making a great bonfire that devours everything. Afterwards there are only red embers and ashes, which are blown everywhere. Now everything is a desert, nothing grows, nothing blooms. The city at night is a screen, a lot of images that flash in front of your eyes. Take a good look at the buildings in the centre. They're pointed-headed monsters. You can see their long arms stretching out, trying to catch something. It's us they're trying to grab. But we're as high and as far away as a cloud. We're on the heights where we can look down on everything, where nothing can touch us. We're the lords of all creation.

# 2

# A Vicious Circle

'It's hard to find a boyfriend these days, there aren't many men left,' a young girl jokes, putting curlers in her hair. The Barrio Popular stretches up the mountain along the haphazard path of an old highway. Thirty years ago, no one would have thought it possible to build houses on these slopes. Now every corner is built on. The first wood and cardboard constructions have given way to brick and cement houses that cling tenaciously to the hillside.

The few streets in the neighbourhood have been asphalted; the tracks which run up and down the slopes have been cemented over. The narrow passageways bend and twist this way and that. To any newcomer, it is like an impenetrable maze.

Noisy children seem to spring up all over the place. They dash about, firing with sticks that are make-believe machine guns. They make the ratatat sound, and their hands shake from the force of the bullets they are firing. They climb aboard their wooden carts and zoom off down the hill... In a corner, some girls are playing 'grown-ups'. They are cooking in pots. One of them knocks at an imaginary door...it's Rosita, the next door neighbour.

'Where's your husband?' she asks.

'He went off with another woman and left me all alone,' the housewife replies.

The young boys walk by in their glowing T-shirts: bright red, orange, green, yellow; they wear medallions round their necks, on their ankles; all of them are in Reeboks or Nikes. The girls wear skintight jeans, slit-sleeved tops that show their bare midriffs. They walk with an inviting click-clack, laughing without a care.

Although most of the stores have steel shutters, the calm appearance of the neighbourhood can deceive the visitor. Everything seems quiet. The ice cream parlours play tangos and local Colombian songs. Street-sellers offer food. Mothers are carefully hanging the washing out on terraces and balconies, tending the tubs in their gardens, or sweeping the streets and pavements so that 'no one can say that being poor means being dirty'.

At six in the evening, all those who've been out struggling to make ends meet return to the neighbourhood. Women who work in rich people's houses, or in dress workshops. Men who do back-breaking building work. The street-sellers... They all clamber aboard the crowded buses. At about the same time, the women who sell themselves for a living, those who work in bars, the night watchmen, are leaving for work. The night people.

The faces of old people are framed in windows. These are the country peasants who founded the neighbourhood against all odds. They are quiet, lost in thought. According to them, life nowadays is not calm like it used to be, everything has changed. In the last few years, the war has affected every corner of the neighbourhood. A war of youngsters, scarcely more than kids. Gang warfare that has left so many dead that everybody has lost count of the numbers.

A war which spawned another one. One fought by a group of locals in the neighbourhood, who decided they'd had enough of 'being pushed around' and who decided to 'clean the place up', to get rid of the gangs that had taken it over. Two years ago Don Rafael, whose whole life has been one period of violence after another, got together with Angel, a young man of 25 who sees himself as a Robin Hood, and the two began the self-defence of the neighbourhood. They got all the locals together, collected some guns, set up a system of payments, and began their operations. Three, four, five youngsters have been killed on each block... shot by the gangs, shot by the law, shot by the self-defence groups, shot by...

☆  ☆  ☆  ☆  ☆

Don Rafael lives up one of the narrow alley-ways, two blocks below the main street. He's got a bit of a store in his house, serving people through his window. On the wall hang adverts and warnings that are never heeded: 'No credit today, come back tomorrow', or 'credit for anyone over 80 who brings his grandfather with him'. His house is full of paintings and little decorative touches. In the cramped living-room is a picture of a far-off spot, with swans, a luxury mansion and huge trees, an orange-streaked sunset. Vases filled with paper and plastic flowers stand on tables covered in woollen mats that his wife has made, embroidered in patterns she learnt from her grandmother.

'I've lived my life, but people still want me to do things for them,' Don Rafael says in his odd slow country drawl. He has the face and hands of a peasant. His hair is turning white, he wears a long-sleeved shirt and plastic slippers. He is carrying a book by Vargas Vila: 'Aura or the Violets'. Vila's always been his favourite author, he reckons.

'If you want to hear about violence, I'll tell you the story of my life, or that of any of the people round here. We have always had to live with violence; there have been very few periods of peace. Each and every one of us is a whole novel.' Sometimes serious, sometimes laughing hilariously, lighting one cigarette after another, Don Rafael begins to tell me the novel of his life.

☆  ☆  ☆  ☆  ☆

## Don Rafael

Two years ago, when we decided to set up the self-defence group, I called on the priest and told him how things stood. He already knew what was going on, how we were suffering from the violence.

'Father, you know we've tried time and again to talk to the authorities, but we've got nowhere. These youngsters are going to finish us all off if we don't defend ourselves,' I told him.

'Don Rafael, I am a priest, and I preach peace. But if I am attacked, I have the right to defend myself. Everybody has that right,' he said, so it seemed to me he accepted our idea.

I wanted to ask him what he thought because even if you're not exactly the most religious person, you do believe. All my life I've been a Catholic and a hard worker. I've been all over Colombia, cutting down thick jungle, working as a foreman, a cattleman, a woodsman, a builder, storekeeper, selling things, I've turned my hand to everything. I've had to struggle all my life, to hang on, to keep on going. Always trying to grab that fickle lady money, but she's always slipped out of my grasp. But when all's said and done I'm proud that I managed to bring up my eight children by decent work my whole life.

What has followed me and chased me all over is the cursed violence of our country. And that's stuck closer than an ugly girlfriend. I've lived with it ever since I was a young man. I was born 58 years ago in Argelia. Into a family that was as poor as can be. I got married at 22 and began my wanderings.

First of all came the political violence, which I saw in Norcasia, in the department of Caldas. There were Liberal thugs killing Conservative families, Conservative thugs killing Liberal families, and the army killing both lots. You had to stay off the roads in those days, just about everyone was ready to slice you to bits, you had to stick to the countryside, keeping out of everybody's way.

I remember one day I was going to cross the bridge over the River Manso, on my way from Norcasia to La Dorada. I was on my guard, because you always had to keep a look-out, and I heard noises and people talking. I jumped into a ditch by the side of the road and looked down at the bridge. There were soldiers on it, with about 30 prisoners. I could also see a local man, Señor Gonzalo Arredondo, sharpening a machete by the side of the bridge. Shortly afterwards I saw them pick out one of the prisoners and get him to put his head on the rail of the bridge. Then this Señor Gonzalo chopped at the back of his neck, sliced his head right off. They did that with all of them: their heads fell into the river, then they heaved the bodies after them. They stopped from time to time to sharpen the machete. When I saw the heads, the bodies, the blood dripping off the bridge, I was sick to the stomach. Cutting someone's head off means you leave the body without the soul. The head is where you have your intelligence, your love, your eyes: you are your head — the rest is important of course, but you can still live without a hand or a foot, but not without your head. That's why a lot of people, when they think about revenge, think of chopping the head off. I've heard that's what General Maza did, in the days of the war of independence from Spain. Once he waited on the bank of the River Magdalena for the Spaniards who were fleeing in defeat, rounded them up, chopped their heads off, and threw them in the river.

Don Gonzalo was a woodsman, a decent hard-working man. It was the violence that made him completely heartless, like so many others at that time. One morning, he went off early to work in the woods, and when his sister didn't appear with the breakfast as usual, he went back down to his house to see what was wrong. Apparently what he saw was like the Day of Judgment: his mother and father were dead on the verandah, his sister was tied to a post; she'd been raped. His little brother, who was lying desperately wounded in a wooden crate, told him what had happened. Gonzalo was left with nothing in the world except his vengeance. From that day on he followed the army wherever they were pursuing the different bands. Every time there was someone to be killed he asked to do it so that he could avenge his blood. He went through the whole region, from Dorada to Puerto Berrío, searching out bandits. They say that one day he went out alone to get one of the biggest killers in the area. He was known as Black Cap, and there was a reward out for him. Don Gonzalo took to the mountains behind Puerto Berrío and followed his tracks. He could move around just like a mountain cat; they even said he had a pact with the devil. One day he caught up with the band by a river in the middle of the jungle. Black Cap was leaning against a tree; the others were happily bathing. Don Gonzalo crept up on them, making sure he was hidden behind the tree. When he reached the bandit leader, he lopped his head off with a single blow, and ran off with it before the others even had time to blink or react. Four days later he arrived in Puerto Berrío still clutching the putrefied head. He claimed his reward, got drunk for a week, then set off after more heads. That was the life of Gonzalo Arredondo after his family was massacred: cutting off as many heads as he could.

In those days, there was violence and there was magic. There were people who knew secrets, who turned themselves into animals to escape their enemies, so that even bullets that had been blessed had no effect on them. I met a man called Eliseo who knew about witchcraft, and he said prayers to protect me. But things got so bad that I decided not to wait around to see if his prayers had worked. I think they have though, because I've come through a lot of risks unscathed. I followed my father with the family. We went to Cocorná, here in the department of Antioquia. I bought a plot of land, or of jungle more like, which was in the back of beyond. It took all day just to get there from the town. I buried myself there for a good long while, but eventually I got sick of it. The very same day that a five-month-old boy of mine died, killed by that cruel jungle I reckon, we packed up a few things and set off, without the first idea of where we were going to end up.

I ended up in Medellín. A friend helped me, and I started working as a contractor for the Land Credit Institute. That was the first time I lived here in the Barrio Popular, when it was just starting. We made these hills inhabitable thanks to all our joint efforts. We organised people with the help of the church and Community Action. Those were good times; everyone helped each other and there was no hatred.

After that I left with the same company to go to work in Chigorodó, in Urabá. Things looked good, and I was earning decent money, so I stayed there. A month later, I sent for my family. The business I had going was to buy plots of land, build a house on them, then sell them off. I managed to save up a bit of capital. I already had eight kids to look after.

Then I had some problems with the business, and found myself farming again, on some land I still own, on the other side of Apartadó, high up where the mountains start. My eldest kids and I turned it into a real gem of a place. We planted cocoa, bananas, maize, and got a few head of cattle. The earth there produces everything, it's really bountiful. You have to work hard, but at harvest time it's a treat.

But then the violence hit Urabá. People have always been killed there, but in the past few years I've seen and heard things that are every bit as cruel as the violence I lived through earlier. Once when I was sick, I went down to the hospital in Apartadó. I waited for about two hours, and when I was about to be attended, the woman doctor said she couldn't see me because there had been a massacre and she had to go and help the wounded. She asked several of us to go with her, because there were so many of them. I agreed, but I never thought we'd find what we did. We left on the Turbo highway. Near Currulao we headed down through the banana plantations, as if we were making for the sea. When we reached an open piece of ground at a place called Punta Coquitos we came upon a whole crowd of people. As we got

closer we could see what a butchery there'd been: there were
more than thirty bodies, ripped to pieces by machine-gun fire.

Relatives were pressing round the bodies; it was a
heart-rending scene. The buzzards were already circling
overhead. There were troops and police asking questions:
what time did they come here, how many of them were there,
did they identify themselves at all...until one of the women
started screaming:

'Why are you asking all this? You know exactly how it
happened,' she shouted, without looking at them, then went
on crying and hugging one of the victims.

A few days later there was another massacre. A whole lot
of people were killed on the La Honduras and La Negra
estates. I didn't go there, but according to the news there
were forty dead. Everybody said it was a paramilitary group
from Puerto Boyaca who had done it.

So many people get killed in Urabá. Sometimes by the
guerrillas, sometimes by the army or the paramilitaries. I
remember one night when a group of these paramilitaries
showed up at the El Osito estate, shouting 'Long Live the
FARC! Down with the military!' But the real guerrillas knew
about the operation and were waiting for them. There was the
most almighty gunfight, with lots of people killed.

Another time we were bombed. There was a demonstration
in Apartadó, and all the peasants came down from the hills
for it. As they came past the estate, the guerrillas were waiting
for them, and they organised a political meeting. I went along
with two of my boys to hear what they had to say. There
were about a hundred peasants altogether, in the banana
plantation. Suddenly someone shouted:

'The army's coming down the highway!'

The guerrillas ran off to take up positions in the irrigation
canals on the plantation. They shouted to the rest of us to
disperse. A few minutes later the bombardment began. We
were walking along among the rows of banana trees when
we heard the sound of helicopters, then some tremendous
explosions. We scattered in all directions. Because they tie

up the banana trees with nylon ropes so they won't fall down, we men had to hack our way through with machetes, while the women and children followed on behind. I thought it would be a massacre, but by some miracle not one of the peasants was killed. Several guerrillas and soldiers did die though.

Whenever there's a clash like that, the army comes round searching, asking questions. One afternoon we were out on the porch enjoying the breeze, having a chat. It must have been about six o'clock, when suddenly soldiers appeared from all sides. They came into the house and searched everywhere.

'We know that you lot collaborate with the guerrillas, those bandits,' the patrol leader told me.

'No sir, the problem is that we're stuck here like a mule with two sets of reins: first we're pulled one way, then the other, and we're the ones who always suffer the consequences,' I said very calmly, so that he had no excuse to get angry.

That's the truth of it anyway: if the guerrillas arrive and ask you for a favour, you have to do it. And if the army comes, you have to pretend you know nothing at all.

The fact is, I've never had any problem with the guerrillas. They always behave themselves. They were often around; they talk to people and organise them. At one point we started a self-defence group. There were a lot of robberies; houses broken into, and cattle stolen. So the guerrillas organised a group to clean up the region. They won't tolerate any drugs or crime. For a while, things went well: not so much as a cent was stolen, you could leave the farm and know it would be safe. But then things started to go wrong. The members of the self-defence group thought they could get away with anything, and started to push people around. They reckoned that because they had weapons and were backed by the guerrillas they were something special. They would get drunk and demand that everyone pay them tribute. One night, one of them got into a local farmhouse, wounded a boy, then killed the father because he wouldn't let him mess around with his daughter. It was drink and women that ruined the group. Finally things got too much. When the guerrillas saw the problems, they set up a commission to judge the members of the self-defence group, and finally shot about six of them. After that, they decided to keep an eye on things themselves, and that worked a lot better.

I had to come back from Urabá to Medellín because I was ill with a kind of cancer. I've got tumours in my body. I've had several operations, and I feel a lot better, but I haven't been able to go back to work on the farm. It was very painful having to leave Urabá — it's good earth that gave me a lot.

I've been back here for two years now. I started this bit of a store to earn enough to eat, and sometimes I go back and visit my farm. All my children are married now, so they're not a burden to me any more.

When I arrived back in the Barrio Popular in '88, the gangs were the great problem. Kids you'd known as little boys had turned into thieves and killers. Sometimes we'd say we ought to get organised to defend ourselves, but we never did anything about it. Then one day I was tending the store when a group of them burst in with revolvers and shotguns. They stole some money, the TV, the sound system. Then they left, warning me not to say anything to the police.

'If you squeal we'll kill you, old man,' they said.

I felt so humiliated, my mind was made up. I called Angel, a young neighbour of mine, and told him what had happened.

'Aren't there any men around here any more?' I asked him.

He took me up on it, and that day we killed the first of them. A lot more have got it since then. The gangs were very powerful, so it's been a hard struggle, but we've made some progress. It's a lot quieter round here now.

In spite of all these deaths, I don't feel any remorse. I wouldn't hurt anyone without reason. All we did was to defend ourselves. Am I a believer? Of course I am. My family has always been very Catholic — I've got three uncles who are priests. I believe in God, the Holy Virgin and all that kind of thing. I know the Holy Bible says it's a sin to kill, but that's if you kill other Christians. Here it's animals, not Christians, that we're killing. Because no thinking person would kill a working man to steal his pay and leave his family hungry. Not even animals are that cruel. We defend ourselves like true Christians, and none of the killing is on my conscience. I've never slept more peacefully.

☆ ☆ ☆ ☆ ☆

## The Guerrilla

In 1984, when we signed the ceasefire agreement with Belisario Betancur's government, we thought we should establish camps in the shanty towns. In Medellín we opened camps in Barrio Popular No.2, in Zamora, Moravia, Villatina and Castilla. We carried out political and military training, we gave talks and had debates on different topics, and on the quiet we trained people to assemble and strip guns, to do intelligence work, and to 'liberate' things. When we had our camps we'd go out and 'liberate' food trucks and distribute the food. Then the police would come and the shooting would start. That happened lots of times, until the agreement fell through.

There must have been between 50 and 80 militia in our camp in the Barrio Popular. We split them into groups for sport, political classes, and military training. There were a lot of kids from the streets there, kids with drug problems who we wanted to re-educate and put to the service of the country. We gave more military training to those we thought seemed most interested and promising. We must have trained about forty altogether.

In mid-1985 the government issued a decree banning these camps of ours, because they said we were training guerrillas rather than promoting peace. After that they began to attack us, they raided our headquarters, arrested people, pulled down our flag. Things got so difficult we had to close the camps and head off into the hills again.

Some of the kids worked with us until the attacks — the government terrorism — began, then they got scared and split. Some even went into the hills with us, but others stayed in the city and began to form gangs. They used the military training we'd given them for their own purposes.

One of them was Ignacio, who started the famous Nachos gang. He came from a poor family. He showed up at our camp one day saying he wanted to work with our organisation; he said he wanted to learn, and eventually became one of the most active of all of them. After we pulled out, he began to organise kids for crime, and they started hold-ups and robberies which they said were in the name of the M-19. We formed a commission and went to talk to him. We told him that if he was going to carry on with his activities, he had to respect the name of the organisation. He did carry on, holding up buses, making people pay taxes, but stopped using the name of the M-19. He got kids from the neighbourhood and others who'd been in the camps to join his gang. At one time there must have been about sixty kids. Since then, a lot have been shot, others are in jail for a good many years, the rest have left the neighbourhood.

Three of the Nachos gang came and joined us in the hills. One night they ran off with several heavy calibre weapons. We caught up with two of them before they left the mountains, and they were shot. We found the third one some time later here in the city. He was killed soon after in a gang fight.

Something similar happened over in Villatina. The best known case was the Florez family. Several brothers joined the organisation, then they ran off with some weapons. They began all kinds of strange activities, again saying they were doing it for the M-19. They were extorting money from one of the city's big businessmen. He handed over part of the agreed money, but said that before he gave them the rest he wanted to talk to the commander of the organisation. The

Florez brothers were so taken in by him that all three of them came down for the meeting they'd arranged, over in La Playa avenue by the Sucre highway, in the city centre. All very smooth, the guy began talking to them very politely. A few minutes later the place was swarming with plainclothes policemen, and the shooting started. All three brothers were killed.

Another kid from Villatina who joined the military side of the organisation took two guns. He got together with an ex-soldier, and the two of them began to terrorise the people up in the shanty town. It got so bad we had to set up a commission to look into it. We had to deal with the guy because he wouldn't listen to our warnings.

The same thing happened with a lot of kids. In those days we thought our time had come, we reckoned war would break out all over the country when the peace agreement with the government failed. That was why we didn't think too much about who we were bringing into the militia or the organisation. We were preparing for all-out war, and we did a lot of training and carried out a few major attacks. But not all of those who joined the militia turned to the gangs afterwards. Lots of them were straight and honest, and gave their lives for the people. Lots more who stayed in the city went on helping the organisation. We now recognise that our tactics then were a mistake. A big mistake. We should have given more political instruction and education, and less military training. But that was how we thought in those days.

The EPL (Popular Liberation Army) is responsible as well. When they saw us giving military training, they did the same. They trained kids who went on to start gangs. That's what happened to Montañero, who was trained by the EPL, then went on to form his own gang. There were about fifty of them altogether, in Santa Rita and the Barrio Popular. They did a lot of harm in the neighbourhood, they were really horrific.

There were no gangs before we set up our camps, just a few cheap crooks. Addicts who spent all their time on street corners, smoking dope and listening to music. They'd occasionally hustle people and beat them up in some dark corner, to get money for their drugs. There were people wounded and killed, but only occasionally. Then everybody got a gun, and there was a war. Lots of people got killed. I admit that the camps had something to do with the start of the gangs, but we weren't entirely responsible. They sprang up in parts of the city where there hadn't even been any camps. I think the real reason is the state of our society, the drugs and the influence of the drugs mafia.

Now that we are sincerely seeking peace in Colombia we also have to find a solution to the dreadful conflicts in the poorer areas of our cities. Perhaps we need to organise the young people to do constructive work. Perhaps we should work with children so that the history of violence does not repeat itself endlessly. I was born and brought up in this neighbourhood, so I feel personally responsible for trying to bring peace here. If those of us who were fighting for an ideal finally realised that violence led us nowhere, then these kids who pick up a gun without the faintest idea why should be able to understand that as well.

☆ ☆ ☆ ☆ ☆

Angel looks like a cross between a gangster and an intellectual. Like most of the young men from these neighbourhoods up outside the city, he walks stealthily, with a characteristic cautious sway from side to side. He calls himself a true Christian, a follower of Father Camilo Torres.[2] He says he values people who are not selfish or vain, but work to serve the community.

On the walls of his room are various posters with landscapes and slogans. One of them shows an old oil lamp shining in the night, with the message:

---

2. Radical priest who fought for the ELN guerrillas in the 1960s. Killed in shoot-out with army, 1966.

Even though errors may hurt you,
even though a betrayal may wound you,
even though hope may be extinguished,
even though pain stings your eyes,
even though your efforts go unnoticed,
even though ingratitude is your only reward,
even though everything seems worthless...

TRY, TRY AND TRY AGAIN

Angel, who sees himself as a shy person, who can remember the fears that shadows, ghosts and apparitions caused him as a child, now roams the streets of his own neighbourhood like a phantom. Two years ago, he and four other locals, dressed in black and with their faces hidden in hoods, stole out along the hidden byways at one in the morning to carry out their first mission as 'avengers'. Their victim was a thief who 'terrified the community, an undesirable element'. Since then, many people have felt the weight of their 'justice', in this 'clean-up campaign' that shows no sign of ending.

# Angel

When you put on a hood, it's as if you take on another identity. You're no longer yourself, you only think of terror, of spreading fear in your enemy. As you walk down the street you see everybody run into their houses, windows are shut, curtains are pulled, even drunks sober up as if by magic. All that's left are hidden eyes peering out through cracks at where you're going. They think you're demons from another world. Walking down a street in a hood lets you see all the expressions of terror in man. They're all afraid, even the bravest, toughest of them.

But sometimes, when I'm not caught up in it, I start to think. I stand on a roof-top somewhere and watch what's going on in the neighbourhood, watch the people going by, and think about things. Even though you know why you're doing what you're doing, it does get to you, you feel guilty. So I pray, I ask God to forgive me. You can't help thinking of death, of the life you're leading. When you come down to it, it's a sad life. Even though you laugh, have fun, talk to people, you're sad and worried inside. But since you're convinced that what you're doing is right, you keep on going.

We didn't choose to do this. It was our daily lives that pushed us into doing something so risky. Who in their right mind would want to kill their own people, the kids you grew up with, the ones you played with as a child? To see their mothers suffering, weeping for their children? Nobody likes that. But what else could we do? They had us up against a wall, they were attacking us, killing us, even raping girls. Whenever we looked to the law for an answer, all we saw was cops siding with the crooks, so what could we do? A lot of people left the neighbourhood. They couldn't rent or sell their houses because no one wanted to live here, so they just left. Left to go hungry elsewhere. But it cost us a lot of work and effort to build what we have here, so why throw it all away and start again from scratch?

We grew up here, it's all we have. We came here twenty years ago from Ituango. We built this house ourselves, and I grew up in it with my five brothers. The old man was always keen on the rum, so we never had enough money. I started work when I was twelve. First I was a porter in Flores square, then I was a messenger for a car agency. At first there was only one room to the house, we all slept together, the old folks too. If you look at it now, it seems quite large and solidly built, but you can't imagine all the work that's gone into it. And what people most care for in life is what's cost them most effort, what they've made with their own hands.

At 18 I was caught in a raid and made an army conscript. I did the regulation two years in uniform. When I got out I worked for a long time as a debt collector, then I sold books. I studied at night, and finished my secondary education. I got interested in left-wing politics. Got some ideas in my head.

Then in 1985 the M-19 arrived in the neighbourhood. That was the time they were excited about the peace agreements with Belisario. They drove past one day in a red truck inviting all the kids to join their camps. A lot of us went along, including all the junkies and delinquents. It was something completely new for us: to be able to see the guerrilla heroes close to, how cool!

They gave talks about politics and organised activities with the community. They gave those of us who had joined the militia military and political training. We learnt how to handle guns, to make explosives, to plan simple military operations. Most kids couldn't care less about all the political stuff, what they were really hot on was the military side of things. The EPL guerrillas, who were also talking to the government, started camps too, where they gave military training.

But then the agreements with the government began to fall through. The police raided the camp and took down the flag. They didn't capture anyone because the guerrillas were on the look-out and gave the alarm. The M-19 organised some actions, they had several shoot-outs with the army, then they split for the hills. That left a lot of the militia kids on their own. Only a few went off with the guerrillas, and most of them came back. Some formed gangs to carry on as before. Then the gangs became dangerous. They knew about weapons and so on, so with their shotguns and revolvers things soon got out of hand.

Gangs like the Nachos, the Calvos, the Montañeros, the Pelusos grew up and started to spread terror. Generally there were two or three older kids and a whole bunch of short-assed runts who thought they were killers at 13, 14 or 15, real tough guys. They would extort taxes from people, 2,000 pesos a week from the stores, 5,000 from the buses, they'd stop and search people in the street as though they were the law, they'd hold up goods trucks.

For the next two years there was no stopping them, they controlled the whole neighbourhood. Life here changed completely, everyone shut themselves up in their houses after six in the evening. The gangs began to kill each other, they'd fight over jobs, in vendettas, or for control of territory. Locked up indoors you'd hear them shooting the hell out of each other. The next day you'd hear about who'd been killed: one down by the church, another over in Andalucía, two more outside the school. There'd be five or ten deaths every night.

The only time the law really intervened was in 1987, when they came after the Nachos gang. They shot the two leaders, and arrested about 25 of the hard core. The gang was more or less finished. But even worse gangs took their place, people who were even more bloodthirsty, who killed just for the sake of killing.

I'll give you an example. There was Jairo, who lived up on the hill. One Friday he came back from work, stopped off for a cold beer near the bus station. All he wanted to do was relax a bit listening to the music. But four kids from a gang came along. They caught him unawares and stole 10,000 pesos — his week's pay. When he was walking home he saw them again about a block from his house, and shouted at them:

'You bastards, you'll pay for this,' then ran off.

The four of them followed him home. They dragged him out, beat him up and shot him.

His body was taken to the morgue and handed back to the family on the Saturday afternoon. That night, after they brought the body home, they organised his wake. We were all there offering our condolences, with women praying and the usual holy joes. At about eleven, six guys armed with revolvers and shotguns burst in and made us all stand against the wall.

'Is there anyone here who reckons this prick didn't deserve what he got?' one of them shouted.

I was expecting a massacre. Instead, they threw the flowers and palm branches off the coffin, and smashed down the candelabra. They were screaming and still pointing their guns at us: we were all standing there paralysed, like dummies. One or two women were sobbing, but the rest didn't say a word. They were crazy, they got hold of the coffin and tipped it over. The body fell out. One of them started stabbing it, another put three shots in it.

'Let's see if there are any heroes who want to make something of this,' they shouted, still waving their guns at us as they left.

The kid's poor mother in the middle of all this had to call the police to take the coffin away in a patrol car. She had to finish the wake in the house of a sister of hers, over in Aranjuez.

Then there was a fellow called Alberto who had dared to stand up to them once. They broke into his house, tied him up, then raped his wife, who was six months pregnant. Don Alberto was a decent man, he never had problems with anyone. But they gave him a day to get out of here. He left like a lot of others had to, angry and desperate, but with their tails between their legs.

Things like that happened every day, but the law was nowhere to be seen. Usually they never came up here, and if they did show their faces and arrest a few people, within half an hour they were back again. They paid their way out, then came to get their money back from the people who'd reported them. The cops also used to work with the gangs, you'd see police cars supplying drugs to the dives, or taking their cut. The police sold them weapons and ammo too.

The M-19 had left a self-defence group behind, and I was a member, but we didn't do much. Then one day a gang robbed Don Rafael, and that same afternoon we decided to organise our own defence properly. We got together ten people and talked about the situation. People we'd chosen who we knew we could rely on, who agreed that they'd help and we'd all work anonymously. We did our first job that week. We killed a useless punk, down below the house here. After that I got in touch with some others who had joined the M-19 militia, and other kids from around here I knew I could trust. I told them what was going on, they wanted to join in, so we really got started. People were so angry, things took off from there.

We got hold of some black suits and hoods, and began to patrol at night.[3] At first everyone was terrified: who wouldn't be, seeing phantoms like us? They thought we must be from the DOC, the F-2, or the military intelligence brigade. But when they saw we were killing the thugs, the scum, they began to take our side and to help us whenever they could.

We beat the gangs by using our heads, with psychology. We knew who they all were, but they didn't know us. There were a lot of them, and they had guns galore, but we managed to catch them out. We began with four .38 revolvers that friends lent us. Our most powerful weapon was terror. Thanks to the help we got, we knew the gangs' movements, and could pick them off one by one. When we learnt that one of them would be in such and such a place, we'd go get him.

We had a house at the foot of a gully with lots of exits. We'd meet there at night. We'd split up and make our way separately to our destination. We'd put on our hoods and go into action.

'Open up, it's the police!' we'd shout, breaking the door down.

We'd all rush in, take the guy out, and finish him off in the street. We got one after another. We killed the ringleaders, the ones with the worst records. We'd give the kids who'd just got into the business a warning: either they went straight or left the neighbourhood. If they ignored the warning, we went for them.

We organised a support network throughout the neighbourhood, so we had information on everything that was going on. We knew exactly what the gangs were planning. They were so unsuspecting that they would even say to us: tonight we're going to get the Capuchos, we'll be waiting for them in such and such a place. They didn't suspect a thing. Later things got really hot, it was all-out war. The

2. The gang's name became the Capuchos, from the Spanish for 'hood'.

gangs tried to hit back at us, but we were too strong. There were about 200 of them, well armed, against us. But arms aren't everything, you also need information and people's support. We began to work in the daytime as well as at night. Some of our group had been recognised, so they didn't bother with the hoods any more.

We collected more guns with each operation and our group grew. One night we hit at several of them. They began sleeping in groups in houses, so we got bolder in our attacks. In the end, they found things so tough that all those we hadn't already shot hi-tailed it out.

Then we started on the drug dens, and we're still hitting them. First of all we send a warning to the guy running a place. If he doesn't react, we give him a taste of what's to come: we go to his house and shoot up the front, or throw a grenade in his yard. If that doesn't work, we break into the place, take the money, the drugs, and all the stolen property, and give them one last chance.

We know that sometimes people are forced into dealing out of need. But trying to solve the problem for one family ends up hurting a lot more. The shit they sell is the main reason for kids becoming criminals, it really ruins them.

We've found ourselves up against the army and the police several times. Not because we wanted to, but because that's how it turned out. The worst fight was one Tuesday night about a year ago. We were headed for a pool hall down near the old police station. We were at the door when a police patrol arrived. Two kids who had been posted on the street corner started firing. The other five of us up ahead took cover behind some walls and covered their retreat. We were stuck there, unable to move because the pigs were pouring lead at us. All we had were hand guns. Then the army arrived, and things got really hairy. The soldiers always carry Galils, it's difficult to get anywhere near them. I thought: if we stay here fighting it out we're done for, we'd better risk everything on trying to break out. What saved us were the grenades we always carry with us. They're pretty powerful, but above all they make an incredible noise. So we started throwing them, and pulled out. They were still firing at us all the time, but we reached a bit of waste ground and then slipped down into a gully. One of the kids was killed, another wounded in the leg. That was the worst moment we've had.

With all this fighting we managed to get rid of the gangs from the neighbourhood. It was a bloody struggle, but the whole community has supported us. There was no other way, no one else was going to do it for us. The government hasn't done anything, nor have the guerrillas. I think those left-wingers talk about military questions in the abstract, but they can't solve the simplest problems. All the guerrillas vanished from round here as soon as things got tough. They abandoned the people. That's why we don't believe in the left. They do a lot of talking in their little groups, but they've nothing to say to ordinary people who are the ones suffering. I was in one of their groups for a while. We spent all our time in meetings talking about imperialism, the bourgeoisie, exploitation, the class struggle and so on...a lot of blahblah, but we never got to talk about how things were in real life. So I decided I might as well spend my time as I'd done before, having a few drinks with my girlfriend on Saturdays, and I never went back to their meetings. They said I was misguided, but I preferred it that way. Now they're criticising the work the self-defence group does, but they've no right, they upped and left just when they were most needed. If the left had paid attention to what was going on, they could have controlled the whole place.

Now everything is fine here again. It's a good neighbourhood, the people are friendly and helpful, they're decent and hard-working. Here, particularly in this part, there's been no mention of robberies for a good long while. At the weekend sometimes we have street parties, everybody has a drink peacefully, we talk and dance a bit, with no problems. It's great.

Of course we've had our fair share of problems in the past. It's been a bitter war, with lots of complications. Some relatives of the people we've killed who knew who we were have set the law on us. The police have raided our houses and followed our tracks. We had to do something, so we told the relatives: either keep your mouths shut, or get out of here. Those who didn't listen had to leave the neighbourhood.

Some things have got out of hand. Some of the kids from the self-defence groups have turned into hired killers. When someone has killed say twenty people, they won't take anything from anybody. Killing criminals makes them happy, they're like psychopaths. There was one — he's dead now — who reckoned he needed to kill at least one guy a week. He was turned that way because of what a gang did to his family. One day when they were all watching TV, a group of four hoods armed with pistols and shotguns broke into their house. The kid managed to escape up to the roof and could see what was going on. He had to watch while those guys tied up his old folks and raped his sister, who was only 16. Then they went off with the TV, the sound system and the liquidiser. After that, he swore he'd get his revenge: that's why he joined the self-defence group. He said he wanted to kill every last one of them. He'd shoot all the junkies and petty crooks he came across. When we tried to stop him, he left the group and formed his own gang so he could go on killing, but he went way too far. In the end, he was killed in a gunfight with a gang from another neighbourhood. That was difficult for all of us, we never thought things could turn out like that.

Others have gone to the bad. They feel powerful with a gun in their hand, they get drunk and start pushing people about and thinking they can do what they like. We had to kill two like that because they got together with a gang from another neighbourhood and started attacking our own people. They went around causing trouble, they paid no attention to our warnings, so we had to hunt them down.

I can understand that people need to do jobs to make money. A lot of the kids in the group are looking for work but never find any. Look how things are: we've all got brains, strength, we're young and healthy, but we go from door to door asking for any job at all, and there's nothing. People can't let themselves starve. They have to find money where they can, but I say to them: go get the money where there's plenty of it, not here in the neighbourhood where we're all in the same boat. Let's take it from the rich who've got plenty of it. That's why the self-defence group has nothing against doing jobs, just so long as they're not harming our own people.

The group has got so big it's hard to control sometimes, but we've set strict rules to try to avoid problems. I wish there was peace so that we could leave all this shit behind, so we could all lead quiet lives. But almost every day new gangs spring up in other neighbourhoods, or even in this one, and they threaten to bring back chaos. We can't relax, because that way we'd lose all we've gained so far.

Further up the hill there's a new group, about a dozen kids aged around 14 or 15. They're being led by a few of the leaders left from the old gangs, who're out for revenge. They say they'll pay them to get rid of us. They're already up to their tricks. We've decided we can't let them get too far, let them grow too much, because that would make things difficult. I think we're going to have to go get some of them. That hurts, killing kids from your own people. We know the problem is a social one really. That unless a lot of things change in this country, more and more young kids are going to turn out as delinquents and killers. It's a vicious circle, and though sometimes we think everything's calmed down, it never lasts. Up to now we've dealt with more than a hundred kids from the gangs, and there's no sign of it stopping...

# 3

# The Fixer

### Julián

It's pure luck I'm alive, I was in the middle of all the shit for a long time. Now I go to the cemeteries and see people I knew all over the place. A lot of hard men I knew personally.

I got into all the violence after I finished school. I spent about six months looking for work but there was nothing. The old folks didn't get at me for it, they even gave me money, but it gets you down still having to depend on them at that age. I had some friends who were doing jobs, I used to talk a lot with them and we'd go to parties together, they were good fun. But I'd never wanted to do any jobs with them.

They knew they could trust me, so one day they asked me to stand guard for them while they were hitting this guy. On a highway out of Medellín. I was in a parking lot with my walkie-talkie in a bag. I had to keep my eyes open to warn them if there was any sign of the law. Everything went fine. I earned my cut. I did the same job a few times, and gradually got drawn into it. I was glad to work for those guys, they knew what they were doing. They looked after everyone in the neighbourhood, they didn't cause any problems. I never saw them pull their guns out in the street or threaten anyone. There must have been about 15 of them in the gang, they were all good guys, not cheap street-corner thugs. No way. We did robberies for money. We did hold-ups in factories or banks, or contract jobs — bumping someone off, or collecting payments. Most of the gang are feeding the worms right now. There are only about three of us left alive.

At one time we had to get out of the neighbourhood because the shit hit the fan with Rocky's gang. They were a bunch of assholes who thought they could run the place. They wanted everything for themselves. They killed innocent kids for no reason and started messing round with the girls. Then one day they came for us. We were in a bar and they came and started foul-mouthing us. Mono, our leader, told us all to cool it to wait and see, but then the next second he pulled his gun on them. He shot one of the bastards and then everybody started shooting. Five guys were wounded, including two who had nothing to do with anything. It was a miracle no one died.

That was how the war with Rocky's gang started. There were a lot of them, and they were well supported, so things looked bad for us and we had to quit. The law was on our tail as well, so we found a house over in La Floresta and holed out there for a few months.

There were eight of us. Mono, the leader, was a good guy. He had a real air of authority, he could control all of us. I learnt a lot from him. He studied engineering at the university for a while, but since it was money he was really after, he soon took up crime instead. Antioquia University was shut for months at a time in those days anyway, so he had to find some way of surviving. He always dressed impeccably, only said the strict minimum, and the women were mad about him.

Pato was the one who liked killing. That guy had an itchy trigger finger, he always wanted to shoot. They made him part of the gang because he never missed. Mono managed to keep him from going round causing trouble. We used to help Pato write love letters to a girl he'd picked up on a trip to Cali. She led him a real dance. Every three or four weeks, he'd be off to La Sultana to see his girl. We used to get together to think up romantic ideas for him to write. He was the most religious too. He had a tiny statue of the Virgin in his room, and every night he'd light candles and pray to her.

'Holy mother of God, mother of us all, don't let me get put away, help me when I'm in a tight spot,' he'd say.

Sardino was only 16. He was the artist in the gang. Whenever he had any money he'd buy canvases and paints. He really got off on his landscapes. He learnt to paint in classes they gave down at the church hall. He used to phone up his girl and give her the most incredible speeches. He wasn't putting it on, he really did love her. We'd laugh at him for it, but he couldn't have cared less.

Costeño was a guy who came from Montería, but had been in the neighbourhood for years. He spent his whole time doing crosswords. They were his passion. He bought newspapers and magazines just for that. He was always in a good mood, cracking jokes, singing songs, dancing about. In the end I suppose he was the sanest of us all.

Football crazy is what the other three — Belleza, Pedro and Caremalo — were. Nacional here, Medellín there, Higuita this, Higuita that... they never missed a game. Every Wednesday and Sunday they were at the match. Sometimes the whole gang would go, with a few girls as well. We'd watch the game then go for a few drinks in a bar along Colombia street.

Some days we spent the whole time playing cards or dice. Everyone would cheat and then get into tremendous fights until Mono came along and sorted them out. I used to fill in time reading all those far-eastern ideas — you know, the ninjas, meditation, mind control, things like that. I've always got a kick out of that.

Most of the time we just sat around. Our contact used to appear every so often at the agreed time. He'd roll up in a Mazda with his ma, an old timer of about sixty. He'd give us the details, and some money on account, then split.

Whenever we were going out on a job we'd put the bullets to warm in a pan first. Mono decided who was to do what, if we had to go by car or on motor bikes, where the job was and

who we had to hit... everything always worked out fine. We
never had any problems. It was all well planned. All the shit
came from other gangs, from enemies who had it in for us.
But as far as business went, the gang came out one hundred
per cent.

After we'd done a job we'd make sure we had a good time.
We'd give some dough to our families and friends who were
in Bellavista prison. Then we went out to buy clothes. After
that, liquor, coke, and women. Then we'd party all night. Or
else we'd go to a disco. We could spend 100,000 pesos or
more in one night. We'd go wild until all the money was
gone and we were broke again. Then we'd wait for the next
job.

We had to leave the house in La Floresta because there was
an old witch opposite who was a regular loudmouth. She
spied on us day and night and even squealed to the police.
We only escaped by pure chance. The cops showed up one
Thursday afternoon. Most of us were out getting details for
a job, and the rest of the gang were in the city centre. Costeño
was the only one left in the house. They raided the place,
searched everywhere, but all they found was one Colt .45.
The pigs were real mad because they'd expected to find lots
of shit:

'You motherfucker, where's the coke?' they shouted at
Costeño.

They took him away. When we got back an old fellow who
runs a store on the corner and who was a friend of ours told
us what had happened. We hi-tailed it down to the police
station, and found someone who'd fix it with the police to get
him out.

After that we came back to the neighbourhood because we
reckoned everything had gone quiet. Rocky's gang was just
about finished: the cops had arrested seven of them, and
Lucas' gang from a nearby neighbourhood had done for a few
more. So each of us came home as quietly as we could. Then
about three weeks later, Mono got killed. One Saturday night
he was standing out on the corner having a drink and listening

to music. A black jeep came past slowly and there was a burst of machine-gun fire. Mono was killed, and so were two ordinary working kids who had nothing to do with anything. That was the end of our gang. Everyone thought they could be the leader, and it didn't work. In the end, we all went our own ways.

I was fed up with all the deaths, so I took the old woman's advice and got a job. I married a girl from the neighbourhood who I'd known for a while. We've got on real well, and now we have a little girl. I did a course in computer programming, which is something I really like. But with the marriage and all there wasn't enough money, so I started looking elsewhere again. You can't live on 60 or 70,000 pesos — I wasn't born to give myself a hard time.

So in the end I lined up three kids from the neighbourhood to hit the payroll in the firm where I was working. It was an easy job because I had all the information. But one of the kids, Orlando, got himself caught because he was new to the game. He was still running scared even when he was four blocks away from the place. A couple of cops thought it looked odd and stopped him. Three million he had, but still he ended up in the slammer.

That evening I came home as usual, sure he wouldn't rat on me. But in the middle of the night the F-2 guys came knocking and took me away. Straight to jail. I tried to find out what had gone wrong. The kid insisted he hadn't said a word. And since he was inside as well, it was probably true. He'd wanted to do the job in the first place.

It was at the first court hearing that I realised what had happened. I asked why I was being held:

'Señora Rosa Bustamante has testified that you persuaded her son to carry out the robbery,' the clerk told me.

So that was it. On the day of the hold-up the cops had visited Orlando's house. His mother got scared and gave the game away:

'My boy would never have done that, it must have been Julián,' she told them.

So I talked to Orlando and made it crystal clear.

'I know you're an honest guy who wouldn't do me any harm. When your ma comes to visit on Sunday tell her to go to the police and say I've got nothing to do with this — if not, you'll be responsible for what happens'.

The kid was scared witless because he knew if he didn't do it he was a goner. So he told his ma what to say. That same week Doña Rosa came down to the court and said she had no idea who her son's accomplices were. That she'd been desperate when she'd mentioned my name, but she had nothing against me at all. They were left with no proof and no witnesses.

I spent six months in Bellavista while all the legal stuff was being sorted out. A lot of smoke: crack and shit all the time. I spent all the money I'd saved in there. It's cheaper to live like a king in Coveñas than to be in Bellavista. While I was there I became friends with two guys from the same block who were in for a murder. A couple of crazies who'd lived a lot. They got out before me because they paid bribes. We agreed that as soon as I got out too I'd look them up.

So as soon as I was free I joined up with them. Not in a gang, we were too old for that kind of shit. No, we're fixers, if you get me. Not like fixing people up with women, but go-betweens. We're in touch with the people who want a job done or have information for a job, and we also deal with the gangs, we know who we can call on.

We work out what has to be done, how much it should cost, how difficult it might be. Then we choose the people to do it. We hire the kids for the job and pay them. If it's something big and risky, we take a hand ourselves. Usually though we find kids from the streets round here. It's easy enough, there are kids desperate to do anything.

A lot of them think killing people gives them class. They're really speedy kids, sometimes they don't even want paying if they think they'll get in with a big boss. Someone takes them on, encourages them, then has got them where they want them. They give them guns, or lend them one. Then they call in the favour: 'I helped you out, now it's your turn to do something for me'.

These kids are Rambo robots. When they're told they have to prove themselves by doing a job they'll do anything to show how good they are. They get high and kill. They'll kill anyone, however tough they are. They would even kill their own boss or anyone with a grievance. You have to remember that absolutely anybody, however evil they might be, has someone who will be angry if they're killed. And in this world, enemies are enemies. When someone's angry like that, and wants to spill blood in revenge, they'll search and search until they get it. I know of some real tough guys who've been killed by those kind of punks.

You have to be careful with kids like that. They may do you a favour, kill one of your enemies for example, but then they'll come and tell you: 'That's one stiff you owe me'.

Some of them behave OK, so you pay them and become friends. But others latch on to you for everything they can get. They start with their violence, so you have to chop them down. Punks like that don't last long.

We don't like to work with junkies who'll do anything for a bit of money, because the day they're offered enough they'll turn against us too. We prefer reliable kids, there's no shortage of them.

We don't like to have a regular group either, it doesn't pay. You have to spend a lot to keep on five or ten kids. Only a guy with a lot of dough can run an organisation like that, he has to hand it out all the time to keep everyone happy. What we do is have one or two regular colleagues, then hire others when necessary.

What the cops say about gangs of hired killers is pure TV fantasy. Things aren't like that, there's no regular structure. They're lumping together the people who work directly for Pablo Escobar[4] and all the others who have nothing to do with him. Everyone respects Escobar, because he's helped

4. Medellín drug cartel boss now in jail.

people round here and because his associates pull a lot of strings. But there are a lot of independent operators too.

This is how it goes. There's a small group of guys who deal with the big boss men — who of course never put in an appearance. These guys deal with the leaders of the gangs, and then it's up to them to choose the people they want whenever there's a job to be done.

The people who began this used to be kids from the streets round here, just ordinary kids. I grew up with them, playing marbles, baseball, and other games in the street, we used to go on school trips together to Barbosa or Girardota. Usually they were the leaders, the ones who organised things. Great sportsmen, interested in athletics, basketball, football. Some of them were university students, they were smart, used their heads. They got into the business about eight years ago. They did the first jobs themselves, and made their pile. After that they preferred to find others to do the work. This is the job to be done, they'd say, here's the information, here's his daily routine, his photo. Then they pick the people they want, tell each one all they need to know, and that's that. A lot of guys do their bit without ever knowing what they've got into. They only know what they're told.

These guys have been good leaders, they've done a lot for the neighbourhood. Whenever they could, they'd hand out 200 maybe 300 bags of groceries down at the church. At Christmas they'd buy 15 or 20 pigs, close off the streets, then hold parties for everyone. They helped kids who were studying: 'Oh, so you haven't got any running shoes, look here's 30,000 pesos, go buy yourself a pair.' That's why everybody's on their side, they've always supported the neighbourhood, and helped people in need.

They're no show-offs either, they're very discreet. Of course, sometimes they get out of line. Once I remember one of them, León he was called, was drinking with friends and got completely high on the booze and coke. He told his best friend to have a drink too.

'No León, thanks but I'm not in the mood,' his friend said.

'Nobody says no to me,' León answered, and shot him dead right there and then.

When he woke up the next day, he was horrified at what he'd done. He kind of went mad, he started banging his head against the walls. He spent about a fortnight going round completely filthy until he gradually got over it.

Usually though these people are very straight, they behave themselves. In the end they were forced to leave the neighbourhood because they were being chased by the police. Now they have their apartments and their farms elsewhere.

Once they caught one of them with some evidence on him, and put him in Bellavista. But three weeks later he was out again. It cost him fifty million pesos to fix it. Enough money to satisfy the devil himself.

Those who work for them have got it made too. There's lots of 18-year-old kids round here who've got luxury flats in El Poblado, farms, cars, motor bikes. The only problem is that very few of them live beyond 20 or 23 to enjoy it. They earn the dough, then their families are the ones who get the benefit.

But a lot of those who got into the business later on weren't as straight as the first guys. Some of them were worthless thugs. They didn't have any self-control, they went round killing people at the slightest provocation, because someone looked at them in a certain way, or didn't look at them. They're the ones who ruin the business, who create all the shit.

That's why there are people being killed all over the place. Take a guy I know, Faisán, for example. His old woman was killed for revenge by another gang. He got blind drunk and started shouting: 'Why did those pricks kill my ma, what had she ever done to anyone?'

The other gang split, so Faisán killed one of their sisters in reprisal. Just to hurt them. He said that if he shot them straight out it wouldn't be painful enough. But even so it didn't bring his ma back, and he's still destroyed inside. Killing relatives has become common nowadays, but I don't agree with it. If they can't get you, they take it out on one of your family, they have to pay for it. I reckon you should settle scores directly. Kill me if you like, but leave my family out of it.

It's the new kids who are the most trigger happy. You can see them on the street corners waiting to be offered a job. They'll do anything for whoever pays them. They'll chew anybody up and spit them out just like gum. They become such hoodlums that they see killing as a sport, not a business.

I've never had any kind of blood lust. To kill someone I need to be paid a lot. Sometimes we work for guys we never get to meet. They send a messenger who gives us our instructions. For example, we might go up to Barranquilla and spend a whole month waiting for the hit, then come back without having done a thing. You still get everything paid, the best hotel, all expenses paid. But other times everything goes OK.

Killing becomes a routine. The easiest is when you kill someone who deserves it, who's a thug. Or people you don't know. I'd think hard before I killed anyone I'd worked with or knew personally. Not because I'm yellow, you get used to killing. But it's not good to make enemies all over the place.

What I do is completely different from the street-corner gangs. I live at home, with people who have nothing to do with the business, I don't cause any trouble. If someone wants a job done, they know where to find me. They explain what the job is, how much they're paying, on what terms. You think it over and tell them if you're interested or not.

I've grown out of my crazy days. At my age, with a wife and a kid of my own, I want to take things easy. Growing up, getting experience, makes you change. There are some guys who want to be bandits all their lives. They want to be famous killers, they want people to go down on their knees to them. But I say that if I'd wanted to be famous I'd have become a singer or an actor.

That's why the work I do now is not killing people, it's more often hold-ups and stealing cars. For example, you steal a car, change its plates, get a new set of papers, and you're made. You can get the papers for a car more easily like that than if you have to queue for them. Another deal is to buy a wrecked car, steal another new one of the same make and model, then refit the wreck with all the new parts. Or you can sell off the parts, but then the other guy makes all the profit.

One of the big bosses who imports dump trucks hired us one time. 'I need five new trucks. I'll pay you a million each one,' he told us.

So I discovered a place where they had plenty of smart new dump trucks. A company that distributed building materials. It was easy. I ordered a load of sand, and gave them an address to deliver it to. I'd already hired someone to hijack the truck and drive it to a car park for me. I gave him 200,000 pesos. Between us we got hold of five dump trucks. Before you could blink, they resprayed them, changed the engine number, the plates, and drove them off to another city. Price as new: eight or ten million. Those are the best kind of jobs. You don't make all that much dough, but it's easy money. You just have to supervise things.

We also do robberies, to get more money. One day for example we went over to a mining region to steal ten kilos of gold. In the end, we only got our hands on one, because half an hour before we showed up the mine owner had sent the other nine to Medellín. We stuck a gun to his head.

'Either you hand over the gold or you're a dead man, we're not leaving empty handed,' we told him.

The old guy was shit scared, he handed over all he had left and almost went down on his knees so we'd believe him.

'I sent all the rest off and only kept this one kilo because my father always told me that a miner who doesn't keep some gold on him is a dead man.'

And it's true — if he hadn't taken his pa's advice he'd have been a goner.

Before I used to spend everything I got. If I had two million pesos, I'd call some friends and we'd all go off to the coast for a couple of weeks or a month to live it up like Arab sheikhs. Until we'd spent every last cent. When I came back I was as

poor as before I'd started. Then I'd wait for the next job.
That's how I lived for several years. But now I've got two
apartments, a car, and I keep plenty of ready cash handy. The
idea that you have to spend it all then wake up the next
morning asking for credit in the corner shop is a load of
bullshit.

If I can get my hands on a big job, I'll retire. A job that pays
thirty or forty million. That's what I'm after at the moment,
the big one. Lots of my friends have done it. Now they've got
the dough invested and they live the good life. Of course you
get used to action, to things happening, but maybe it's time
to settle down. We'll see.

In this country everybody has to look out for themselves.
There's nobody straight or honest. Look at all the politicians:
what we do is kids' stuff compared to them. They clean up
millions just with a signature. They don't even have to work
for it.

The law's the same. Take the police for example. They're
crooked, they're just crooks in uniform. If they frisk you and
find a gun, they demand money. Then they've got your
details, and every so often they turn up for their cut. Those
guys eat so much, they must have four stomachs like cattle.

And don't talk to me about the guerrillas. A lot of the kids
who were at school with me started out as revolutionaries,
but now they prefer the easy life. They spent a few years with
the guerrillas, then they set up their own gangs and devoted
themselves to getting rich quick. That's why I reckon that we
all have to look out for ourselves. You can't trust anybody
else to help you. No chance! It's everyone for themselves.

# 4

# University of Evil

In the entrance there's a huge painting that's been blurred by rain and time. Some naked, proud-looking men are playing a game of basketball. In the background, a big round sun shines on the green of meadows and gardens. A slogan underneath reads: 'It is the man who enters here, not the crime'.

Bellavista, the prison for the legal district of Medellín, was finished in 1976. Its proper capacity is for 800 prisoners, but for several years now it has held an average of 3,000. This is the most violent prison in the whole of Colombia. In its short history it has beaten all records: the worst overcrowding, the greatest number of escapes, the greatest number of murders, greatest number of riots, greatest number of sacked warders... the first real massacre in Antioquia was committed against seven Bellavista inmates. In Machado, a group of hooded men stopped the van which was transferring them from the courts, lined them up and shot them. A 'clean-up' group claimed responsibility.

At the end of 1989 and the start of 1990 a series of events took place in Bellavista which propelled it onto the front pages of all the newspapers. A mutiny left thirteen prisoners and three warders dead. A grenade thrown from block eight injured forty prisoners in block four. Then 350 warders went on strike. They claimed that the prisoners were better armed than they were, and called for troops to be sent in to carry out a general search.

None of this was new. Each time there is a serious incident the government promises an investigation, drastic measures, changes in the prison staff, a reduction in the number of prisoners, but nothing ever really gets done.

To reach the prison blocks, a visitor has to present his ID card and a court authorisation or 200 pesos at each control point. There are five of these. The first is at the main gate. The second is fifty metres up the driveway to the prison building. This is where they put the first stamp on the visitor's right arm. The third check is where the queue starts between the prison wall and a metal fence. The fourth is in the entrance to the prison itself, where guards in tiny rooms like bathrooms search through belongings and put a second stamp on your arm. The fifth is when they take your fingerprints, keep your ID card, and stamp you for a third time.

Then you have to pass through another five doors to get to the cell blocks. You go down a long passageway with grimy walls until you reach the sixth, where the prisoners play football and basketball. From here you can see the watchtowers spaced out along the wall surrounding the jail. The first altars to the Virgin of Mercy appear, decked with flowers. Faces pressed against bars, hands thrust out to you with innumerable requests: 'spare us some money, friend', 'don't forget me', 'remember I used to live near you', 'God will repay you', 'anything you can spare, buddy'.

You also see the long line of prisoners queueing for their food. There is a huge din as the poor in the prison file past with their brightly coloured bowls to receive rations they would prefer to avoid. Wafted on the breeze are dense smells of food, dank corners, leaky pipes. The smell of prison clinging to your clothes.

On visiting days, Block Two looks like a park in a small town. Prisoners and visitors sit at tables in the dining areas to catch up on the latest news: what's become of the old woman, what did the judge say, what's the lawyer's opinion.

The hum of voices mingles with the noise from five or six radios going at full blast. Surrounded by candles in one corner is another statue to the Virgin of Mercy, the patron of prisoners. Some inmates offer handicrafts they have made, holy medallions or carved wooden Christs.

The blocks which make up the prison are four storeys high, divided into wings. Some of the wings in the second block are named after neighbourhoods in Medellín: Guayaquil, El Poblado, Laureles. Others are called Kennedy, the Vatican, the Dollar. When you want to visit someone in Bellavista, you have to know what block and what wing he is in. If you can't find him, you pay a 'loudspeaker' who will bring the prisoner for you in a matter of minutes.

The stairways are decorated with more images of the Virgin and paintings: contract killers firing from a car at a passer-by; a burst of machine-gun fire from a motor bike at a Mercedes Benz; a gangster fighting hand to hand with death.

'You survive in here only if your mouth doesn't say what your eyes have seen,' says Mario, stretched out on his bunk. Behind his head are a print of the Virgin, a small picture of Christ, and a photo of his mother. On the wall opposite, pictures of pin-ups from some magazine display their charms. To his right, scrawled in large print, is a prayer to God the Judge: 'Lord, protect me from my enemies. If they have eyes, may they never see me. If they have hands, may they never get hold of me. If they have feet, may they never catch me. Let them not take me from behind by surprise. Let me not die a violent death. Let my blood not be shed. You who know everything know of my sins, but also know of my faith. Do not abandon me. Amen.'

Mario is 23 years old now. By the time he finishes his ten year sentence he will be 30. He plays with the cross around his neck and begins to tell his story, the drama of prison life.

☆ ☆ ☆ ☆ ☆

# Mario

When you get to Bellavista you need two things: money to pay the authorities to put you in a good block, and friends inside waiting for you so that you don't get eaten alive by the pack. From then on you have to show you're tough and not let anyone pull anything on you. If you let them get away with it once, they'll never stop.

I was lucky to have both things. I managed to do a deal with the screws so they put me in Block Two, where I had an old friend from the gang waiting for me. He was well in with the boss man on the block, and that's the key to getting on in here.

It's the boss men who run things. They decide what goes, what the punishments are, they are the law. They're the ones who control the drugs and the money, so they're real powerful. Nearly all the fighting in here is for control of the sale of drugs, because whoever does that has got it made. The vast majority of prisoners are addicts. They take cocaine, smoke crack or marijuana. A block of marijuana no bigger than a speck is worth about fifty pesos. A bundle of crack with twelve cigarettes in it costs 1,000 pesos, a single cigarette a hundred. A line of coke, which is nothing at all, sells for 500 pesos.

The guy who controls the drugs controls the junkies; he's the one with power. The real addicts, who we call spiders, are willing to do anything so long as they get their supply. They are the stooges, the ones the bosses use when they need them. They do the killing for them. They kill anyone who gets out of line, who doesn't pay for his drugs, anyone who squeals or whose life has been bought.

'I'll buy so-and-so,' some guy inside or outside prison will say.

'How much will you give me for him?' they ask.

They strike a bargain, and the next morning there's a dead body in the jail. From outside they want to punish people who've betrayed them: rats, you know what I mean? People who have done wrong or who know so much they're better off dead.

Sometimes there are whole chains of revenge killings. You have enemies who are after you, and you haven't the faintest idea why. You have to stay sharp because when you're least expecting it you can find yourself caught up in some complicated game. I was a marked man once. I got wind of what was going on and went up to see the boss man and my friends. In the end the guys cooled it. It turned out that a new arrival who had a grudge against me told the boss in his block that I was a cop. So the boss set things in motion and found someone to do me in. You can imagine, everyone here hates the cops. I tried to sort everything out, and since I had friends to back me up, the boss man realised he was wrong. So the other guy ended up dead. He had to pay for lying to the boss. They stuck him like a pig, then cut his head off. You don't forget favours like that. That's why you tell your friends: if you're in a tight spot, all you have to do is whistle and I'll come running.

Whenever there's a sneak thief in a block — someone who steals things he finds in the prison — they are punished too. The punishments fit the crime. It's the boss man who decides if it's to be a thrashing that leaves him in bed, a beating with sticks that leaves him in the hospital, or a stabbing that leaves him in the funeral parlour. And if they are to die, they do just that — lots of people know what's going to happen, but they keep their mouths shut, otherwise it's their turn. Then there's the sound of people running up or down the stairs, like a herd of cattle or something, and they stab and stab until they're exhausted. They've counted up to 180 stab wounds in one body. When they kill someone on the top floors, they throw the body into the elevator shaft or down the stair well. Sometimes the infirmary people get to them, but it's rare that anyone survives. A body with that many holes in it soon gives up the ghost.

When a prisoner knows he's going to be punished, he tries to reach the cage, which is a small cell at the entrance to each block. But often the warder won't open it, either because he thinks something strange is going on, or because he's afraid he'll be the one to pay for it. And the investigations into the murders always come to nothing, because they're done by bands of up to forty people. That's why the bodies end up cut to ribbons. So who can be held to blame? If one person is accused, he can argue it was self-defence. If you know that you're a marked man, and you know who's going to do it, you have to get in first. God helps those who help themselves.

The very least that can happen to anyone caught stealing is for him to be thrown out of a block, which makes it very hard for him to find a place anywhere else. The bosses have got it all agreed between them.

All those who have nowhere else to go end up in what we call Guayana, which is like a prison within the prison. They're cells with no light that measure about four metres by two. Ten or twelve prisoners are put in there, so they can't all lie down even. They have to piss and shit in plastic bags and throw them out into the corridor. Once a week or a fortnight maybe they're taken out and given a bit of sun. Just by looking at someone you can tell they've been in the Guayana. Their skin is so pale it's almost transparent. And the tunnel is what we call the worst part of the Guayana, like the hottest part of hell. It's a slimy wet place where all the shit runs through. That's where the dregs of all Bellavista end up, the absolute scum.

There are all kinds of blocks here, though of course you're not really safe in any of them. You always have to be on the look-out. Block ten is for prisoners under 18, and it's one of the most violent there is. That's where most of the rapes take place. It must be because kids miss sex the most. And since like the women in the Buen Pastor prison they're not allowed any visits from the opposite sex, they have to bugger each other. At any rate, every newcomer gets done over. First they soften them up: 'come over here with me, you'll be fine with me friend'. It's all lies: 'hey look, let's pawn your running shoes then on Sunday at my visit we can get them back with the money I'm brought'. Then when Sunday comes round,

'Would you believe it, I didn't get any money at all!' They try it on with every newcomer, and if they don't fall for it, they beat them up, steal all they have, and bugger them right there and then.

The best-kept block is number nine, where the girls are. Some of those queers really look like beautiful women. If you met them in the street I'm sure they'd fool you, they really do seem just like gorgeous females. If you didn't know what they had between their legs, that is... they like to be treated as women, they do themselves up fantastically, with hair-dos, strapless dresses, miniskirts or tight-fitting trousers. Some of them are really sought after, they charge a lot for their services. People in different blocks want sex with them, so they bribe the guards and they let them through. And they're not ones to let themselves be insulted in any way, they're as tough as they are sweet-looking. You have to be careful what you say because they come at you with everything, they're not scared in the least.

Prison plays tricks with everyone's sex life. In this damn place you end up looking oddly at everyone: the only way you're saved is if your wife or girlfriend doesn't abandon you. Or to have enough money to pay 500 or 1,000 pesos for sex on a Sunday, when it's visiting day.

In here you find every kind of perversion, abuse, prostitution and venereal disease everywhere. When people realise someone's given them a dose, they want revenge. The very least they do is kick the person out of their bunk, so they have to find somewhere else to sleep. Diseases like that are common, and they're very hard to control. Most of the women who visit on Sundays are prostitutes, there's about a thousand of them. Some guys run the prostitution business. They put one or two whores in their bunk, and hire them out by the half hour. You can't imagine how busy it is all day. Then there are a few rare women who come regularly each Sunday to offer sex. They visit two or three yards giving pleasure to the prisoners that nobody comes to see and who haven't got any money. It'd all be very romantic but for the goddam diseases they spread right and left.

The special yard is for the rich prisoners, the ones with lots of money. They live like kings. On visiting days, that's where the best women go. Beautiful chicks. That's the yard with least problems, because they have the money and look after themselves. But they don't always get away with it. One guy turned on them just recently. Who knows how many millions he got for shooting one of the bosses three times in the head. They had to transfer him to another jail, because they knew he'd get it. But that didn't save him. They've already killed his father and three brothers, and the whole family is threatened. They'll get him too, I'm sure. It may take a while, but they never forget something like that.

A few days ago there was a real fight. Someone threw a grenade from yard eight into yard four. There was a tremendous explosion, about forty people were wounded and sent to the infirmary. The quarrel came from way back. The bosses of the two yards were enemies from outside, and they brought the fight with them into jail. They were also fighting for control over the drugs market in here. One of the bosses had people working in the other yard selling drugs, and that started the problem. There had been several incidents, and things were really tense. Then one day the prisoners in yard eight were playing football and the ball landed in yard four. They picked it up and punctured it, and returned it along with an obscene message. That made things even worse. Everyone was getting worked up, and then came the grenade. Some guys from the fourth were waiting to ambush prisoners from the other yard when they went to get their chow. But then they threw the homemade grenade from yard eight, and in the explosion all those from yard four were hit with bolts, nails, bits of metal. One of the wounded lost a leg. Innocent and guilty alike get hurt, but if you're in a yard you have to stick by the others whatever happens. If you don't, you lose points and you've had it.

Nothing happened after the bomb. The only thing was that a big-wig came down from Bogotá, from the Prison Department. He got together the two boss men, Tarzán from yard four and Jairo from yard eight, and got them to make their peace.

They were worried because when they searched an old woman who was visiting they found a grenade in her vagina. They thought there was bound to be a massacre. They only discovered the grenade because she hadn't done a deal properly. You can bring anything in here if you pay for it. There are revolvers, submachine guns, gunpowder, dynamite, everything, you name it, in the yards. How does it get in? By bribing the guards, that's how, they're so greedy for money.

Money opens any door to bring things in or smuggle them out. The guards have got it well organised. You can pay to get in without an official pass, or to get through the search they do. Inside the prison, you can pay to go to another part of your yard or get from one yard to another. Or for example you can hand over a hundred pesos to stay in your bunk all day. According to the regulations, everyone is supposed to be outside in the yard from seven in the morning, when they have the roll-call, until four or five in the afternoon. But those greedy pigs make sure they get their share every day. To pay for a particular bunk can cost anything between 20,000 and 200,000 pesos, which is what Freddy, Gonzalo Rodríguez Gacha's[5] son, paid when he was in here. It's the best bunk in here, very quiet and nice.

You can get bottles of rum in here for 6,000 pesos when it's cold or 10,000 when there's a party on. Drugs do the rounds in every yard. The pigs know all this is coming in: the weapons, the drugs, the drink. They keep their mouths shut.

The guards' strike began because a while back they were asking the authorities to search all the yards. They said we prisoners were better armed than they were. That's not true, though we do have enough to defend ourselves. But the

5. Medellín ddrug cartel boss, killed by special police unit in 1989.

guards don't have the strength to demand things, they caved in quickly. The Elite Brigade of the police searched all the yards, but all they found were handfuls of blades, razors, guns and knives, the sort of thing everyone has in here. Look at what I keep with me. It's enough to kill anybody. I made it in one of the workshops and paid a guard 1,000 pesos so I could bring it to the yard.

A few days after the search, in one of the yards they began to show off their guns to the guards in the watchtowers.

'Come and get them, you bastards,' they shouted, holding up their revolvers, pistols and a submachine gun.

It's because there are so many good hiding places in here, no cop or guard could ever find them.

Even if they did manage to get all the guns out of the jail, that wouldn't solve anything because the guards themselves would let them back in. They earn peanuts, so if a guy offers them 200,000 or 300,000 pesos to let a gun in, they sell themselves at once, they get greedy. Can't you see the paunches they have, from all the money they've gobbled up?

There are only a few days when the look and the atmosphere of this hole changes. That's on feast days in honour of Our Virgin of Mercy. It's as if even the foul smell disappears then. We kill a pig, cook a proper fry-up, and relatives come in with special dishes so that everything seems different. We make beer from maracuya, yeast, banana and blackberries. It smells glorious and tastes divine. Of course it also gives you damn awful diarrhoea, but who doesn't reckon that an afternoon of happiness is worth a bit of a shit? If you have money, you can buy rum and you can buy coke or any drug you fancy, or rather any drug you can afford. If I haven't got enough for a few grams of coke, I buy some dope, but I won't touch crack.

The governor allows bands in, and we have fun. A real party. Of course, there are some prisoners who refuse to dance, no one can get them up on their feet. That's because they reckon it's bad luck to dance in prison: everyone has their special beliefs and superstitions.

All of us prisoners believe a lot in Our Virgin of Mercy. In the Old Man as well, but mostly in the Virgin. When it's the feast days, we decorate the pictures of her that are all over the jail. We fix up the frames, paint them, and put candles round them. The Virgin is our queen. That's why the prisoners have tattoos with her on, because they believe so much in her. They also have other tattoos: scorpions, dragons, hearts with slogans, but it's the Virgin who is the most popular. People pray to Jesus as well, but Mary is the mother of God and no-one is more important than a mother.

The feast days end with the game of football that the prisoners play each year against the Nacional or Medellín team. During the year we play a league between the different yards, and the winners get to play the professionals. People go crazy to play with the stars of Colombian football: with Leonel, Higuita, or Uzuriaga. Or if you can't play against them, at least to get a look, to watch how they perform, to see their class.

Here in yard two there used to be a boss who had a music group, a real good guy he was. He ended the celebrations last year with a serenade. He went round all the wings of the jail playing whatever they asked for, and of course the inevitable one: 'The Prisoner' by Fruko:

I'm singing to you from jail
Wilson Manyoma's the name
The world I live in
Always has four corners
And between each of them
Life is always the same.
There's no sky for me,
no moon and no stars,
the sun never shines.
everything is dark around me.
Black is my fate...

Can you imagine listening to a song like that in the middle

of the night after a day of enjoying yourself? It's too much. You're lying there with your blade in your hand, just waiting for the butchers to come for you, staring at the darkness, imagining you hear voices and strange noises. Your spirit sinks, you can feel the prison bars inside you, you feel so bitter, so abandoned and alone. That's why I think night and day of getting out of here, I'm trying to find a way and I'm sure I'll find one. That's why I pray to the Virgin Mary to ask her help in getting me out of here: 'Remember, Holy Virgin Mary, that it has never been known for you to refuse help to anyone who turned to you for your protection and succour. Encouraged by this we pray to you, and though we are weighed down by the burden of our sins we make so bold as to implore your favour, you who take the side of sinners and are the succour of all Christians. Holy mother of God, do not reject our humble pleas, but forgive us all our sins, give us the light and the strength to confess freely to them all, give us the courage to always believe in God's grace, and with your aid win eternal salvation. And if it will help our redemption, we ask these special favours of you: that I may soon emerge from this difficult period of my life, that you bring me freedom and that in your name, Our Lady, may God's will be done in all things. Amen.'

☆　☆　☆　☆　☆

Mario Ramírez was tried for the crime of murder on the third floor of the old National Palace. The courtroom was big, cold and dark, with plain dusty walls, old desks and benches that looked as though they came from a church. This is the courtroom for the Fifth Criminal Court of Medellín. Quite a few kids were there to see the famous judges, gavels in hand, dressed in their black robes and stern-faced. Just like in the films.

'He doesn't look like a judge,' one of them whispered to a friend.

It was true. The judge looked more like a retired civil servant. He was tall and moved clumsily; he was balding and seemed to have more wrinkles than years to his name. He swore in the jury and began the proceedings, as if this were another routine task to be performed, like a teacher beginning a lesson. He ordered the clerk to read out the details of the case, and went off to have a coffee.

The state prosecutor, a small, thin man whose face was pockmarked with the signs of youthful acne, came and went as the charges were being read. He was wearing a grey suit and a smart tie. The public in court noted with surprise that whenever he crossed his legs he showed a pair of shiny shoes but no socks.

Mario's mother María tried to follow the list of charges. The clerk rattled through the many pages at great speed.

'The accused, 1.60 metres in height, wavy brown hair, regular eyebrows, narrow forehead, coffee-coloured eyes, straight nose with broad base, olive-skinned, well-preserved teeth...'

Mario's father, brothers and nephews were also in court. So too were some of his closest friends, a fellow prisoner who had already got out of jail, plus neighbours and others from his part of the city who, although they did not know him well, were grateful to him for having killed 'Chorizo', who they had thought for a long time was the neighbourhood's worst enemy.

Doña María tried hard to keep the faith, to believe that the judge would understand that her son was basically a good person and that he had a right to go free. But her hopes dimmed when her son's replies to questions from the judge and the state prosecutor were hesitant. Mario could only give confident answers to the questions put by his own female defence lawyer.

As the state prosecutor began his speech, a storm began to beat against the old windows of the courtroom.

'My intention, your honour, is to prove categorically,

beyond any reasonable doubt, that Mario Ramírez was responsible for the murder committed...'

This elegant little man, wearing no socks and appearing not to amount to much, grew in stature as he spoke to the jury in a loud and imposing voice, delivering his words as if this were a major trial. All the public supporting Mario felt dismayed.

'There is evidence which leads us to affirm that this crime is related to earlier ones. In our view, Mario Ramírez is guilty of the murder of another three members of the Los Platanitos gang which took place early one morning last May. But since we have not gathered sufficient proof of those murders, I will concern myself only with proving the accused's guilt in the crime which is now before the court. Throughout the introduction to this case you will have heard the names of two people who have never attempted to lead the lives of law-abiding citizens. They belong to two shady gangs. Roberto García, alias "Chorizo", was with the Platanitos. The accused, Mario Ramírez, belonged to the Escapularios. The crime, your honour, revolves around the question of who was to control the supply of drugs in their neighbourhood of the city...'

In their minds, the public accepted or rejected the arguments put forward by the prosecutor in his imposing, silky tones. Everything he said was an outright denial of all the defence had argued. Doña María, previously unaware of all the details, began to piece things together and began to realise painfully what her son had become. She began to ask herself again the questions that she had often asked him: 'Why? What had he lacked at home? Who had set him such a bad example?' Once again, she could come up with no answers. She remembered all the efforts her husband, a driver in a government agency, had made to try to give his children a future. She remembered all the sleepless nights she had spent, her struggle to make sure that her children had everything that could possibly be offered them by a poor family such as theirs.

'I therefore ask you,' the prosecutor went on, 'to find the accused guilty of the crime of murder against Roberto García, known as "Chorizo". We are bound by duty and by law to respect human life, and in this sense the life of the deceased is as valuable as anyone else's in this country. It is the duty of our nation, which I represent here today, to ensure that no crime goes unpunished, not even those carried out by individuals in the name of justice. To allow any citizen to take into his own hands the responsibility for punishing those whom he considers criminals is to promote barbarism...'

These words, which sounded new and strange to many of those in the public gallery, were part of a well-known script for the judge. He showed it by his attitude, walking from his seat to the door, peering out into the corridor then sauntering back, as if he were waiting for the end of a long speech.

'That is why I ask you to show no leniency in the sentence you are about to pass. All the evidence clearly shows that what we are dealing with is a typical case of murder for money...'

By the time the defence lawyer began her summing-up, there was no hope left for Mario. Juan, a neighbour of the family and a lifelong friend of Mario, was perhaps the only one to understand the logic behind the state prosecutor's argument, because he had studied for several terms as a law student. To all the rest of Mario's neighbours and family the inevitable guilty verdict seemed not only unjust but incomprehensible.

'If the person killed was the worst kind of scum, why should anyone have to pay for killing him?' one of them wondered as they left the courtroom.

☆ ☆ ☆ ☆ ☆

## Juan

I've been Mario's friend all my life, we grew up together. But I didn't realise precisely when it was that he changed. I'd see him around, up to his tricks, nothing special. Then he became like another person, completely full of himself. I think it was after he killed for the first time. That was when the real change happened. It shook him up. He told me he'd been scared stiff. I never thought he'd be capable of it. It affected him a lot.

It was one Monday. He was told he had to kill a guy. He was scared, he felt a chill in his bones, but he agreed, he'd do whatever they asked. He couldn't refuse. He couldn't appear to be a coward. He'd already got a reputation as a tough guy. So then he was handed his victim in a house in Itagüí. He put him in a closed room. He was a young man, about 20 years old, who was blindfolded and didn't say a word the whole time. He had been wounded and beaten up. Mario took the call confirming the order to kill him. He was scared witless, and wanted to back out. He had always thought that if he had to kill, it would be in a shoot-out, like in the movies. Or like in his friends' stories, when they talked of gun battles and heroic deeds. While he was loading his 9mm pistol, he looked inside himself, saw himself walking a dark hillside surrounded by noises and strange-shaped shadows. He heard, or imagined he heard, cars pulling up outside the door. He waited, his gun ready, for them to break down the door or to give the order to open up. But there was only a stubborn silence, as if the two of them were alone in the whole world.

When night fell, it was time. He lay down on the couch and lit a cigarette. He remembered his brother, the youngest of the family, who is only five now and has always been his pet. He imagined himself throwing the dead body on a waste lot and escaping as fast as he could, pursued by the police. He saw his old woman's face framed by locks of hair, with her dark, inscrutable eyes. He closed his eyes and felt his body was floating in the air. He could hear children laughing in the street outside, as if they were far away.

He stood up and then, as if a strange force had taken hold of him, he went into the room, shut the door behind him, and pointed the gun at the guy's head. The shot and a hot surge that spread up from his finger through his whole body sent him spinning into a huge, endless abyss. He fell to earth in a nightmarish, desert landscape. Seconds, minutes, hours perhaps, went by. He gradually forgot his fear and felt his own strength grow. He had done what he'd set out to do.

At nine that night he arrived at the ranch in Sabaneta and calmly told them how it had gone. That was the first time he got paid real money, about half a million pesos. They ended up getting drunk and sniffing coke all night long.

That's how he described how it felt to me the first time he pulled the trigger. From that day on I knew for sure that fate had taken him down a different path, and that he'd never find his way back. I know a lot about him because he and I grew up together, we've been friends all our lives. And although Mario chose a very different destiny, we still get on. Everybody has to live their own life.

We always went to school together. After school we'd ruin our shoes playing football in the street. At night we'd roam up and down the hillsides imagining we were heroes, having a great time playing at cops and robbers, waging war, playing hide-and-seek. We got up to all sorts of tricks, smashing lights, sticking chewing gum onto front door bells, picking on Tonito the Grouch, calling him names so he'd chase us with his stick shouting insults.

At weekends our families would go on picnics together. We'd walk up the valley of the Santa Elena river when it was still clean and fast-flowing. We'd climb up to a spot called La Pradera, where there were ponds and fields to play in. Our parents would chop wood and make a fire to cook a stew. We'd spend the whole day up there. So did about half of Medellín. It was when we were still kids that we saw the first victims of violence. One day when we were walking down the road we saw the bodies of two kids, tied hand and feet, who had been thrown into a ditch. That was when the violence started, when they began killing people and throwing their bodies by the roadside. It became a habit, every morning you would find bodies along that road or on the road to Las Palmas.

Things in our neighbourhood were still calm in those days. There were kids who smoked marijuana, a few petty criminals, and two or three of the respectable kind of crooks, who behaved themselves in the neighbourhood, and went elsewhere to commit their crimes.

Mario quit school when we were in the third year. 'I don't like studying, I haven't got the brain for it, I want to work to earn money,' he told me.

No-one could talk him out of it. He was out on the streets for about two years, then he began to work as a mechanic.

We still met at weekends to have fun. We'd dress up smart, and go out in a gang for drinks and try to pick up girls. There wasn't a fifteen-year-olds' party, a first communion, or a school dance that we missed. Whenever there was a chance of dancing we'd be there. In Medellín they dance at any excuse. In our neighbourhood we play the typical music of Medellín, and we like to listen to Sonora Matancera and salsa as well. We'd have a great time and get laid. Mario was the most enthusiastic of all of us, though he didn't have much luck.

'Juancho, I don't know what's wrong with me when I'm with a girl, I don't know what to say to her,' he'd complain. We'd encourage him, and he'd occasionally manage to pick someone up.

But the whole scene in our neighbourhood changed when a black family called the Lalos arrived. They had 15 children, and were on the run from the violence up in the north-east of Antioquia. They were caught up in a feud between families that had already claimed several lives. They decided to come to Medellín, although they went back to the north-east from time to time to get their revenge.

The Lalo family is like a clan. Thirteen of the children are male, and they're all tough nuts, experts in handling machetes or guns. When they get drunk to northern and Mexican music you should hear how they boast about the people they hacked to death in their village. The Lalo family always sticks together, they're never alone. If you pick a fight with one of them you have to take on the whole lot.

On some Sundays they make a pilgrimage to fulfil their vows to the Fallen Christ of Girardota. When they get back at night they go on endless binges. They set up their sound systems on the sidewalk outside their house, and spend the night drinking and listening to Mexican *corridos*. The singer they like best is Juan Charrasquiado, and they always sing:

> I'm going to sing you a song
> of what happened once down at La Flor
> the sad story of a rancher in love,
> a drunkard, a boaster, a gambler what's more...

When they first arrived in Medellín, they looked after gardens in El Poblado. One of the drug bosses took a liking to them and introduced them to the crime business. The first to get involved was Fernán, the eldest. He must be about 35 now, he's a wiry little guy with nothing remarkable about him. At first he did jobs here in Medellín or occasionally went to other cities. Now he goes around ferrying coke for the mafia.

He began to get a name in the neighbourhood because he'd show up in fantastic jeeps, pick-ups, and cars. Huge limousines you could hardly see him in. His appearance changed, he turned psychedelic: he went in for silk shirts in all colours; white, red, or green shoes; dark glasses and smart jackets. He changed their shack into an Egyptian palace: marble all over the living-room and the bathroom, a complete sound system, a TV, video. In the living-room they still have a bleeding heart of Jesus and a big poster of Vicente Fernández with the slogan: 'I'll never run away'.

Of course there are some things they could never change. Their father Don Leonardo struggled for two months with a pair of fine shoes they bought him, but finally he decided he was happier walking barefoot as he'd always done. He only wears them when he goes into the centre of town to buy supplies for the store he's set up in the house. And though the mother Doña Fabiola likes her smart dresses, she found that her life lost its meaning if she didn't cook or do the housework any more.

They didn't have enough money either to change their way of speaking. They still have the drawl typical of people who come from way up in the mountains. But they did learn to listen to salsa music and American ballads. They play them at full blast on their sound systems in the car or in the house, when they're not listening to the Calle sisters and their *carrilera* music.

The other brothers and brothers-in-law went into the business later. They're killers, they earn their money pulling triggers. They have 250 and 500cc motor bikes they roar up and down our narrow streets on.

One time the cops were after them. The police arrived, surrounded the building, and raided it. I call the house a building because it's got about four floors. They were inside a couple of hours and they finally took away two or three of the family. But the next day they were back in the neighbourhood as large as life. Eventually they became such good friends with the cops that one of the girls married one.

So the Lalo family became famous all over the neighbourhood. They were friendly with everyone, but they were tough too, and they often organised tremendous parties and gave their girlfriends incredible presents. We kids in the neighbourhood were friendly with them because we could bum drinks off them and talk like hard men. Sometimes they'd let us ride round in their cars with them. That was a real novelty. But as we grew up we moved on, each of us went his own way. Jairo became a factory worker, El Plaga a salesman, Cafecito became a revolutionary, and is still spouting about it, Oscar went off with the M-19 and is now one of Pizarro's bodyguards. They took all those talks we had as kids about changing the world seriously. Paticas and I went to university. And so on.

The only one who didn't move on was Mario. He left his job and began to do driving jobs for the Lalo family. He did well and got a taste for it. They took him to the outings and the parties they had in ranches outside Medellín. He even used to pick up the women for their parties. He learnt about weapons and how to handle them, and got his alcohol and coke habits.

He transported drugs and guns for them in Medellín, and sometimes travelled to other places. At the start, it was all very easy. Sometimes they came up against police road-blocks, but they always had enough money to get through. Things got more difficult for him when he began to help them kidnap people. They would take him and show him a house. Then he would have to go with a gang and guard it. They would get the person out of the house and he would have to take him to a farm. He would look after them until other people arrived and he could beat it. He was scared and was always glad that he never had to do anything to any of the people they'd kidnapped. He knew there was a war going on, but he had no idea who was fighting it or why.

The first dummy he had to kill really upset him, but afterwards he couldn't care less, he always laughed about it. On the Tuesday after the first time, he arrived home and gave his old man 100,000 pesos to do up the house. He brought more presents for his mother, his kid brother, and for María, a girl from the neighbourhood he went out with. No one asked where he had got the money, but his presents were received without much joy, almost without a word.

Every day that week he invited those of us who were his closest friends to go down to the Brother Inn with him; we were drunk the whole week. And before he had realised it, Mario had spent all his money.

'If you've got it, spend it,' he said over and over, like he couldn't care less, but I knew there was something inside eating away at him.

It was always the same: whatever money he got, he spent.

When they put him in jail, he hadn't even got enough to pay a lawyer.

'Live your life today, even if you're gonna die tomorrow,' he would sing, like the song goes.

It was around then that 'El Cojo', an old crook, came back to the neighbourhood after a spell in Bellavista. He came back such a reformed character that the very next day he started back in business. He stole a TV and a liquidiser from Doña Teresa, who's a very poor woman; he mugged Don Francisco one Friday as he was on his way home from work with his pay, and more things like that... he made everyone angry, and then Mario stepped in.

'We have to get rid of that guy, a rat like him doesn't deserve to live,' was all he said.

On the Wednesday at midnight he and another gang member went to 'El Cojo's' house, dragged him out into the street, and shot him. Mario made no attempt to hide the fact that he'd done it. Some people in the neighbourhood thanked him for getting rid of scum like that.

Then he hit the Platanitos gang, who were about 15 kids no more than 14 or 15 years old. They were terrorising people with shotguns, home-made bombs. They were really violent. They did hold-ups, killed people, shot others, they had no sense of shame. They killed David, a kid from this block who everybody thought a lot of. So then Mario got angry and decided to hunt them down.

That Tuesday evening I was in the Viejo Rincón, a leisure centre here in the neighbourhood, where the old folks go to listen to music like La Sonora, Lucho Bermúdez, Los Matamoros, the La Rosa trio... all the old tunes. Mario arrived with his gang and we chatted for a while. Then they began to plan their attack. They had found where the other gang was holed up. I kept quiet, because the less I get mixed up in things like that, the better. I'm responsible for everything that I do, but I don't stick my nose into anyone else's business. We left the place at about midnight, all of us pretty drunk. I went to my bed, they went to do their thing. I was just settling down when I heard the shots.

Early the next morning the news was on the radio: four people had been killed by a group of unidentified men who said they were from the F-2 police. According to information supplied by the city police, four individuals had arrived during the hours of darkness at such and such a street, house number so-and-so, and had shot and killed four young people who had been identified as... four corpses, in other words.

On the Thursday the news appeared in the crime section of *El Colombiano*, which is like the society pages for the poor people in Medellín. Mario read the article several times. It made him very happy, and the neighbours who more or less knew it had been him thanked him for what he'd done. It's true those kids were an evil bunch, but I'm still keeping my mouth shut about what I think.

Mario's way of thinking was like this: everyone in this country steals, up to and including the president, but they should steal from those who have the money, not from poor bastards. And there I was thinking that our chats as youngsters had made no impression on him.

Mario went on in the same way, on the one hand doing his business, on the other gaining a reputation as an avenger in the neighbourhood. He killed quite a few people. At a rough count, 15. He changed a lot, he even became expert at picking up women. Of course when you have money it's a lot easier. Mario had a motor bike, and a car sometimes, so all the chicks were desperate to go out with him. But María was always his official girlfriend, the one he preferred and loved the most, that's why she waited for him... and though he's taking his time, she's still waiting for him.

The thing is that killing got to be a habit with Mario, he got big-headed about it. He was too cool about it, and that was fatal. He thought he was invincible, in a way.

'Take care, Mario,' we used to tell him.

'Don't worry, I know what I'm doing,' he'd reply.

And it was this arrogance that led to his downfall.

I'll tell you how it happened. Chorizo, the leader of the Platanitos gang, realised Mario was after them, and was on his guard. He was another one who knew no limits, who nobody liked. He was no coward though, and decided to get Mario first. He tried to ambush him twice, he shot at him out of the shadows in the street, but didn't get him. They were in a fight to the death.

Mario spotted Chorizo getting on a bus one Sunday in the neighbourhood. He ran for his motor bike, and found someone to ride it for him. They set off after the bus and caught up with it almost in the city centre. Mario stopped it and got on board, went straight to the seat where Chorizo was sitting and emptied his revolver into him. The guy died at once. But the bad news was that a police patrol car turned up just at that moment, and they caught Mario getting off the bus with the gun in his hand. He went straight to Bellavista. There was no time to sort anything out.

The people in the neighbourhood celebrated when they heard Chorizo was dead. But Mario is doing time for a killing he shouldn't be paying for. About 300 of us here signed a petition. We told the judge about Mario's good qualities and about all the harm the victim had done, to see if he would take it into account.

But the judge wasn't having any of it. That's justice for you. For over a year we were waiting for them to catch that bandit from the Platanitos, but nothing happened, and we had to suffer. Then when Mario does something about it, he gets ten years. I don't understand it.

☆ ☆ ☆ ☆ ☆

## Mario

What gets me mad is that I've been put in jail for killing scum like that. The day I killed him they had a party in the neighbourhood. About half of them had accounts to settle with him, but he just kept on doing more harm. I had been after him for days, but he always managed to escape. That's why I was so pleased when I caught up with him that Sunday, and saw the look of terror on his face as I emptied my gun into him. Killing some people always gets to you. People you don't know, people you are just killing for the money but have no idea who they are. But I enjoy getting rid of trouble-makers, people who show no respect for those they live among. I can't wait to get them.

Now I have to work out just how to get out of here. I've been sentenced to ten years, but I've already done three. That leaves seven. My lawyer says that because this is my first time they'll reduce it a bit more, say two years. And for every three days you work in jail, they let you off one. That means you earn three months' remission for every year you work. So I reckon I have at least another two years in here. That's a long time to be in a coffin like this. Like the song says: 'being in jail is like being crucified, there's nothing but boredom and sadness of heart, if I have to stay here I'm sure I'll go crazy...' You have to try to get out legally, but also the other way too. Lots of people have escaped from here, you have to keep it in mind all the time. It could be your turn at any moment.

The best trick they've ever pulled here was with a helicopter. That was on Christmas Day in 1988. Three crazies hijacked a helicopter that was flying from the Olaya Herrera airport in Medellín to the José María Córdova one in Rionegro. Nobody knows how they got their weapons on board, because there's a permanent group of police who check passengers and their luggage at the airport. A few minutes after they had taken off, the hijackers forced the pilot to head for Bello. He got really scared when they told him to aim for Bellavista. They'd thought it all out, they had flags of Colombia and the National Prison Service with them, and that fooled the prison guards. When they were right overhead, the shooting began, and they fired at the watchtowers. It was like a movie. The prison was full of people who were visiting because it was Christmas Day. We

were all in the yards, and when the shooting started we threw
ourselves to the ground. Five guys were up on the roof of the
art classroom, over in yard six, waiting for the helicopter to
arrive. Nobody knows how they managed to get up there
either: they had to get through four doors to reach that roof.
Four doors that are padlocked and have guards. A few
seconds later the helicopter landed and lifted them off.
Disappeared without a trace. The five who escaped were all
youngsters between 18 and 20. They escaped all right, but
they're all dead now. It may be dangerous in here, but it's
no picnic outside either.

On 18 May last year there was real trouble in here.
Seventeen people were killed, 13 prisoners and four guards.
The plan was to blow a hole in a wall with dynamite so that
a lot of us could escape together. At the same time they were
going to organise a riot in yards two and five to act as a
diversion. But the pigs knew something was going on, in here
everything gets known about beforehand. The time chosen
was two in the afternoon. By half past one, the jail was already
declared in a state of emergency. The man who was supposed
to lay the dynamite saw that things had fucked up and
chickened out. All that could be done then was to throw a
grenade at the watchtower to kill the guard there. Then the
prisoners scaled the walls and climbed down where they keep
the pigsties. The guard in fact wasn't dead but wounded, he
heard them taking his G-3 rifle from him and jumping over
his body, but he pretended to be dead so they wouldn't finish
him off.

When the guard in our yard heard the explosion, he came
running in. He served himself up to us on a silver platter: we
got hold of him and left him like a sieve, then threw him out
into the corridor. In the machine room they killed another
guard. When there's a riot like that, all you hear is one huge
noise, everyone is shouting and making noise with whatever
they have to hand, to scare the pigs. They treat us so badly,
they treat us like shit all the time, so they know that the day

they're going to get it, they'll get it good. That's why they started to run like chickens as soon as the fun began.

We went from yard two to join up with the prisoners in yard six. The guards started shooting at us from the watchtowers. We saw things were getting too hot, so we retreated. Several of my friends were shot.

The army and the police had already surrounded the jail. They began firing at all those who had managed to get over the wall by the first watchtower and were trying to climb up to the Medellín-Bogotá highway. The worst thing was that they shot at prisoners who were out working in the gardens who had nothing to do with what was going on. That was uncalled for, especially those they shot after they had already surrendered. That's what they say happened to El Aguadeño, who was the boss of one of the yards and was the one who managed to get the furthest from the jail. He reached a house, but the police dragged him out and shot him even though he wasn't resisting arrest or anything.

Most big escapes fail because someone grasses. Like when they discovered a tunnel in July '89. Someone told the authorities it was being dug. The guards searched yard five but couldn't find a thing. But at night the patrol heard whispering and earth being shovelled. So they searched again and found the mouth of the tunnel under a bed in a wing of yard five. It was really well hidden. They were digging it with all the know-how. It was well thought out. They took the earth out in small sacks. They got rid of part of it in the drains, dissolved in the water. The other part they stuffed into the hollow walls between the cells. They had dug about five metres of the tunnel, and only had another three to go.

Those crazies would get high on drugs and start shovelling earth. One of them was called 'El Minero' because he came from the mines in Segovia and was an ace at that kind of work. But he betrayed them. They reckon it was him who grassed about the tunnel because he'd had an argument with the rest of the group. That was the second tunnel they've discovered. I've been told that in '86 the prisoners dug another one about eight metres long leading out from one of the jail restaurants, but someone ratted about that one as well.

It's easier to get out of here using the guards. Like the philosopher says, give me the money and I'll make the world spin. Lots of people leave here thanks to deals with the judge or with the authorities in the jail. Things that happen and never get heard about, if you get me. If you've got the money, you can climb out via a watchtower — if you hand them the envelope with two or three million pesos in it, that is. I'm not lying. One weekend, between Saturday and a holiday on Monday, six guys got out into the street. But that did get reported in the press.

There's a whole lot of corruption. On visiting days, despite all the checks they make, several people have escaped. They go through the doors as if they owned the place. At the end of '88 four guys got out during the visits, including the leader of the Nachos. The funniest thing was that they bribed the guards with three million in counterfeit notes.

Whenever things like that happen, they change the governor to see if a new one can bring some order, but he has no chance. The governor has to fight against the guards, the administration who've got their own deals going too, against the prisoners, and against the government to try to get a bigger budget.

The prisoners pay the administration to hide their files. For example, a guy is about to be released for something he did with one court, but he has other charges still pending against him from another one. All that is on his file. Then the file vanishes into thin air, and the jail has only three days to gather all the information again. If they don't, they have to release the prisoner, because otherwise he'll accuse them of illegal detention. In the courts too the papers get lost, because it's the clerks there who are the greediest for money.

Anyone who has contacts and money can get out of here easily. The ones who are stuck are the helpless ones, even if they're innocent. I knew a kid from Chocó who tried to commit suicide twice. He was in here with his brother, accused of armed robbery. They had just got in to Medellín from Quibdó. They met in the Atlántico bar, which used to be on the corner of San Juan and Bolívar. That's where all the people from Chocó who lived in Medellín used to meet up at the weekends to listen to music they liked, *vallenatos* and salsa. A really cool group of blacks. Anyway, the two of them had no money so they decided to go out and rob the first guy who came past. They ran into a guy who was half drunk and stole his watch and a bit of money. But as bad luck would have it, they'd just done the job when two cops turned up and the guy started shouting. He was a good sort really though, and said that if they gave everything back he wouldn't press charges. That's what they agreed, but then the cops started to beat them up, they gave them shit and threw them in Bellavista. The youngest went into yard ten, and he had to undergo the initiation. He was so terrified that he made a noose with the legs of his trousers and tried to hang himself. They got him to the infirmary unconscious and managed to revive him. He tried the same thing again later. In the end, those two got out because the guy they'd attacked made a statement to the judge, and that helped them. But the damage had already been done.

Things like that seem unjust to me. It's only really serious crimes that should land you up in this hell — at least then you know how to defend yourself. But how can they allow a decent person to end up in this hole? A lot of the people in here are honest, but the legal processes take so long that it can take months or years before they get out, even if they've done nothing at all. And during that time they go to the bad, real bad, because decent people don't survive in here. They say that this is a school for criminals. It's more like a university: you can find specialists in every area of crime, it's a real education.

Of course although some suffer and have a hell of a time, there are others who live like kings and never get so much as a toothache. Those are the ones with good connections. They know that their boss outside will look after their family until they get out, and they even get a weekly allowance in here. Tough guys into heavy business who pull a lot of strings. They always live quietly in here though, they never cause problems.

The other ones to watch out for are the 'gringos', the ones who have been abandoned, who nobody visits or sends any money to. They're dangerous because they have nothing to lose. They'll take on any dirty job for a few cents, they'll kill anyone. They know that if they owe money for the crack they've smoked and they can't pay it back, they're marked men. Because that's the law: I'll lend you 200 pesos, in money or drugs, if you pay me back on such and such a day, and on that day you pay me or else. There are a lot of prisoners in the psychiatric wing pretending to be crazy because they know that if they go to any of the yards they're dead men. So to try to avoid paying their debts they pull faces and stare like madmen so they won't have to go back to the yards. Those who don't have a yard like that are called 'refugees'.

What I can't understand is the people who end up liking it in here. I know a kid of 20 who's been in here about 15 times already. Whenever they set him free, he begs them to let him stay. They throw him out anyway, so he immediately starts thieving again so that he can be sent back to this rest home.

How on earth can you get to like this graveyard? You'd be far better off dead. If I get out of here, I'm never coming back alive, I swear it. I prefer to be shot wherever they catch me. The only thing that gives me some hope is my family, especially my old woman. She hasn't missed a single visitors' day since I was dumped in here. Every Sunday she gets up at half past three in the morning to come here. I'd do anything for her. If I get out of this hole I'll give her the best of everything: she's deserved it, the best, no matter what I have to do to get it. That's why I pray every night to the Virgin, to help me here in prison, but above all to get me out quick.

# 5

# A Word in the Midst of Death

### The Priest

Flaco was leader of one of the toughest gangs in the neighbourhood. He was a tall dark-haired youngster aged about 22. He used to roar up and down the streets on his motor bike. I used to see him all dressed up, with very pretty young girls. I remember him well because he knew I was a priest and whenever I ran into him he would look down at the dog he always had with him and say sternly: 'Tarzán, let's you and me go up the hill to smoke our crack, eh?'

He was killed a while ago. The wake and the burial were a complete carnival. The other gang members kept his body in their house for three days. They were listening to salsa, sniffing and smoking, drinking. Finally his family decided to bury him, even though the gang didn't want to. On the Wednesday they came out bearing the coffin on their shoulders. They walked down the streets stopping at every corner as though it was a religious procession. At every corner where Flaco used to operate, they put the coffin down, played loud rock or salsa music, and talked to the dead body. They gradually made their way down here, to the park outside the church. They put the coffin on a platform in a corner, and carried on with their ceremony. Flaco's mother got angry and made them come inside the church. Some of them stayed outside drinking and smoking dope. About 20 of them actually came into the church. In the middle of the mass they put a portable cassette recorder on the coffin and played some salsa songs in his honour. I went on calmly with the religious ceremony, I've seen all they get up to before. They came up alongside the coffin, slapping the sides, and saying to him: 'you're a good guy, we're still with you, you always treated us right...' as though they were at a farewell ceremony for some god or other.

In the cemetery, they took the body out of the coffin and carried it on their shoulders, they shouted wild slogans to it, fired shots in the air, and then eventually buried him. I've seen a lot of strange things in my time, but that burial was the strangest of all.

It may be that a lot of priests, and the teachings of the Church itself, would not agree, but I respect the way that they bury their dead. That is how they react spontaneously, it comes out of their lives and the way they understand things. Other social circles make great speeches or spout political slogans when their leaders die. These lads talk to their dead leader, they touch him, play the music he liked, and it affects them deeply, you can see by their rituals. They have lost their leader, their guide. And even though it may interfere with the traditional religious ceremony, I know they are not doing it to be disruptive.

The gang leaders all have the strangest funerals. While they are alive, they give instructions as to what ceremonies they want, and the records that are to be played. Those leaders, like Flaco, are created by the lead of bullets, by their strength, by heroic deeds. Whoever is best at riding a motor bike, the one who is the best shot and kills the most people, he gets chosen as leader. His orders are not questioned, they're simply obeyed, however absurd they may be. It's the leader who handles the money and the contacts, and the others worship him.

These things are hard to accept, but my role is not to be a judge, or a policeman, but to try to understand their difficult reality and do all I can to change it. Their relation to religion is complicated as well: they sin and make up, as the saying goes. They attend mass, take communion, they make vows, wear religious medallions everywhere and occasionally even come to confession. All this is part of popular tradition, the Colombian people have always been great believers. And these youngsters are too, in their own way. As you can see, today is a day of devotion to the Virgin, and the church is full, the women come, the men, and quite a few of the young folk as well.

A lot of them are gang members. The sons of honest families, who have taught them to respect education and decent hard work. Young people I have known all their lives, who are fine individuals, until all of a sudden they get mixed up in that madness. They're desperate to get a gun and a bike so they can have money, expensive clothes. Their families worry a lot and suffer. Their mothers come and tell me the stories. But sometimes when the kids start giving them presents, they begin to accept the idea. In some households they even support them when they ride stolen motor bikes or sell crack and things like that.

It's very difficult to judge people because they have such uncertain lives. This is a very poor neighbourhood, lacking in almost everything. The youngsters get desperate and turn to crime. And every day they see the media encouraging them to buy only the best — brand-name clothes, to have money, a bike or a car. That's the stereotype that advertising and the mafia bosses have created.

If you haven't even got enough to live decently, if you have no job or earn a pittance, while every day you are being shown what you need to lead the good life, and if at the same time you have the connections so that you can get all that, then it's easy to fall into crime. I know that not all the youngsters get into it because they're going hungry. Some come from families that are quite well-off, but in this neighbourhood the vast majority are poor. The fact is that not even a middle-class family can offer a kid enough money to maintain the standard of living that they feel is necessary. You can't imagine just how much money one of these kids can spend in a week or even in a single night.

A few days ago another gang leader was killed. His name was Jaime, I'd known him since childhood, I was even his sponsor for confirmation. Before his death he'd been living in El Poblado, in a luxury apartment, with his wife and child. He went around in the most expensive limousines. He was one of the few I've seen who really managed to make himself a small fortune. Because for every one of them who gets that far, there are a lot who die on the way. Like most of them, he started off doing little jobs that didn't implicate him too much, but as soon as he started seeing real money he was hooked, and he ended up where he could never have imagined he'd be. He began as a look-out, helping them steal cars, and by the end he was a professional killer.

His family is very decent. His mother is a typical Medellín matron, his father works hard, and the other five children lead honest lives. When Jaime first got started in these things, his mother talked to him a lot. When he carried on all the same, she threw him out. One day she told him that her house was not a hiding-place for criminals. But then later she softened, she let herself be bought by his money and by the presents he brought her. He called her 'the Beauty', and only the best was good enough for his Beauty. Elegant Mother's day parties, with lots of presents, gifts of money, until finally he won her over. She had two masses said for him every month, so that the Virgin of Carmen would protect him. He was very religious too, and almost every week he'd go down to the shrine in Sabaneta to Our Lady of Succour to offer and redeem vows to her. He always brought candles for himself and his family.

I spoke to him several times when he was already up to his neck in it. Obviously I advised him to give up the life he was leading, and he always said that what he wanted was one big pay-off so that he could retire. But the truth is that there comes a moment when they're no longer doing it for the money, they could have million upon million and still wouldn't give it up. They still hope to climb higher, to do even more spectacular things and become even more important in their world.

I visited the family a few days ago to give them my condolences. His mother spoke of him as if he had been a saint. She told me about all he had done for the people in the neighbourhood, the food he had handed out, the poor people he had helped, what a fine person he had been. But she did not mention that he had been shot while he was attacking a police station, with a gang of killers, and on the Thursday before Easter too. That's why they say there's no such thing as a dishonest corpse. The mothers above all try to rescue the image of their sons. Sometimes they invent such good stories they end up believing them themselves.

Jaime's story is typical of most of them. They can't get the fever out of their bones. They're driving a car that has no reverse gear, they're on a kind of roller-coaster that's headed straight for death. Of course I have known some who have repented. I'll tell you about them. I can remember Ñatico, a kid from up on the hillside who came down to the church one day and right in the middle of confession handed me his revolver. He told me he was tired of killing people and doing wrong. He told me, almost in tears, of all the shady things he had done. He had even taken part in massacres. I didn't want to take his revolver, to avoid any problems, but I encouraged him to start a new life. Now he's got a steady job and seems to be doing fine.

I knew another youngster, a drug pedlar who nevertheless always came to mass on Sunday. At eight o'clock mass in the evening he'd be there in a corner at the back with his sisters, who were very pretty girls. He always took communion.

He built himself a real fortress, a house several storeys high, with hiding places and tunnels that led out to a gully. All on the strength of the crack he sold. At first his family was against it, but in the end they were taking turns so that the place could function 24 hours a day. They made a fortune. Then gangs from the next neighbourhood attacked the place several times, so he formed his own gang from friends round here and put bars on his windows, like a pawnshop. People talked about him as though he were a complete Frankenstein's monster. More than a few people died in the battles that took place round that house.

One Sunday I started a campaign, inviting people to speak out about the drug dens because of all the harm they were doing to our young people. I repeated this call at the eight o'clock mass. After it was over, this man came up to me and started telling me all about his life. Of how hungry he had been, why he had got into the drug-dealing business. It seemed strange to me that he did not feel he was harming anyone by selling them crack. He said that whoever bought it must need it, that he didn't force anyone to smoke, and that anyway if he didn't sell it, somebody else would. He seemed to have very confused ideas about it. He even offered me his house as an old people's home. I said he should take advantage of all the money he had saved, he should sell the house and move somewhere else where nobody knew him so that he could start to live a decent life. He told me that was what he was going to do. I haven't heard any news of him for some time now, so I don't know whether he took my advice or not.

One Easter Week a desperate mother came to see me. She asked me to go to her house with her because one of her sons was possessed by the Devil. I laughed, and said I wasn't going because I'd probably die of fear if I came face to face with Satan.

'I want you to take this seriously, Father, you have to talk to my son for me,' she insisted.

So I went to her house and found a youngster of about 18, obviously in anguish and suffering. He was doing his military service and at the same time was a member of the Manrique gang, one of the toughest around here. They had brainwashed him, and had him programmed to kill. Whenever he was on leave from the army, he went off on his criminal activities. Then the gang leader was killed and he gave thanks to God, because he saw a chance to get out of that life. He told me that he'd already tried several times, but they'd always threatened to kill him. He felt that now he could make it, but he wanted me to tell him whether God would pardon him for all he had done. In cases like that I always think that the future is the important thing, to look forward. So I suggested he change his life to try to reconcile himself with God. And he did.

But those are exceptions. Most of these kids pray a lot but continue along the same path. The only weapon I have is the word of God, the offer to change. Sometimes it works, but I don't think their lives can be altered much by sermons. I can see all those young people rushing to the precipice. They know they are 'disposable', that when they join a group they are not going to last long, but nothing can stop them. They start to think of death as something completely natural. I see them at funeral after funeral. Today they are saying goodbye to one friend, tomorrow to another, and the day after... Some days here there are three or four burials, all young men.

They are kids who keep going in the fantasy of always having more and more. They act without thinking. They reckon, or are convinced by others, that they can have and deserve to have lots of money. 'The money's been printed, all we have to do is go and get it,' they say. Once they've started, there's no holding them back.

They talk of the drug bosses as their idols, they dream of working with them, of becoming someone. To achieve that they'll do anything, no matter how absurd. I remember the case of two kids who were great friends who were driven out along the road to Las Palmas. When they reached a lonely spot, they were told to get out of the car and one of them, known as 'El Tigre', was given a gun and told to kill the other one. To show his class, as they say in their language. So that boy killed his best friend just to win points and gain esteem in the gang. 'El Tigre' came to mass yesterday with his group, they were burying one of their group who had been killed by a gang from down below in the city. The ceremony passed off normally. After mass, I stood at the church door as usual to give everyone my blessing. 'El Tigre' lifted off the lid of the coffin and they all had their photos taken with the corpse. They hugged the body, shook his hands, talked to him.

Our world seems totally crazy. On street corners you can see youngsters of 13 or 14 smoking crack and playing with revolvers. They're all waiting for their big chance, the big job, so they can show how good they are and get a reputation. But only a very few of them ever manage to make any money. Normally they just spend all they make, 50,000, 100,000, 200,000 ... if those kids can earn that kind of money in no time, why on earth should they ever want to work in a job for the minimum wage? They find it very hard to fit in to normal life.

It's getting more difficult every day to find a solution to the problem. To start with, because there is no real authority. Nobody respects the police, because they have done a lot of harm as well. I wouldn't say all of them are guilty of it, but many are. Some people say they don't know whether to be more frightened of the gangs or of those in uniform. And they have committed some dreadful abuses. Usually it's against decent folk, because they do deals with the criminals. They arrest youngsters for possessing firearms and haul them off to the police station, but all they do is take a bribe then let them go again. Ask anyone in the neighbourhood and they'll tell you stories of the links between the police and the gangs.

So if there's no law and no justice, what can possibly work? There's always a lot of fuss about poor neighbourhoods like ours, but no one ever decides to do anything about it. Not the government, or any of the political parties, not the businessmen, and I have to admit that the Church has not done enough. There are priests who believe that everything can be solved by moral appeals, but they don't adapt their preaching to real life. Everybody in this country is concerned above all with defending their privileges. Every time a tragedy occurs, the crocodile tears flow. Until now, all you hear are laments, but if that attitude doesn't change, the problem is going to grow to unimaginable proportions. We have to consider the new generations. Just look at the streets, they're full of children; what's going to happen to them?

Lots of young people come to the church asking for help to find a job, but unfortunately I don't run a job centre. That is where we have to start, by offering the chance to work to anyone who wants to. To look after children, really look after them, from the time before they start school, to offer them new attitudes and values towards life. So that they don't learn all they know from the street, because that is strewn with death.

A lot of young people are changing. Here in the parish there are 70 altar boys, 200 in the military band, and a group of scouts as well. Every new group that starts attracts lots of youngsters keen to join. I believe that even the youngsters in gangs have their sense of values and that it is worthwhile talking to them. Whenever I meet any of them, I talk plainly to them, I ask them what they've been up to, what's happened to them, and I tell them straight out that they should think of trying something different. But I'll say again that if these young people are not given the chance to play a useful role, they'll continue to sink into a world of crime.

There are lots of possibilities, and we have to try them all. Most of the people in these neighbourhoods are decent folk, including the youngsters. People who have struggled all their lives, who have organised to solve a lot of their problems, and who still have a tradition of solidarity and neighbourliness. The challenge is to offer them alternatives, and to help them to make them real, to divert them from a path that inevitably leads to death.

The solution is not simply to bring more police and soldiers in, that much is obvious. All this year there have been troops everywhere, but the gangs continue their wars and the young people go on killing each other. You can be asleep at night and be woken by shots. Sometimes I'm no longer sure whether I'm dreaming or it's really true. I go out to my balcony and someone tells me; 'They've killed two more, Father', or three, or four, down on some street corner or in a bar.

I think what we need is proper authority that people can respect. And above all, we need to start up small businesses, family businesses, artistic groups, sports clubs; we need to improve the schools and teaching methods, we need to improve the standard of life all round.

Whenever a group that young people can join closes or is not formed, that means those youngsters are left with only the world of the gangs. We have to snatch the new generation from the clutches of death, that's our challenge... nobody can afford not to face it. In the meantime, my task is to accompany the community — the families, the mothers — in their times of trouble. To offer them my solidarity and my words of hope. Fortunately, the figure of a priest still commands respect. And I use my position to keep in contact with everyone, including the youngsters in the gangs, and to offer them the chance to live.

# 6

# The Rebirth of Desquite

## Medellín at War

Many years ago the poet Gonzalo Arango wrote the following lines on the death of Desquite, a Liberal bandit leader during *la Violencia* in the 1950s: 'I place this rose of blood in one of the eight bullet holes that they shot in the brigand's body. One of these shots killed an innocent man who never had the chance to be one. The other seven killed the assassin he had become... and I ask over his grave dug in the mountain: Is there no way that Colombia, instead of killing all her sons, can make them worthy of living? If Colombia cannot reply to my question, then I prophesy this misfortune: Desquite will be born again, and the earth will be watered once more with blood, pain and tears.' Gonzalo Arango did not live long enough to see his prophecy fulfilled.

Desquite is still dying and being reborn. His soul wanders throughout this country, which has been unable to find peace even for its dead. The violence now is not the same as in the poet's time, but is its continuation. It no longer stalks mountain tracks but has come down into the streets of our big cities. Neither then nor now has Desquite been master of his own destiny. He is still obsessed with death, but his victims are no longer his enemies.

At the end of April 1990, the leader of the M-19 and presidential candidate Carlos Pizarro León-Gómez was assassinated. His death was a repeat performance of a script enacted many times before. A youngster from Medellín shoots a political leader although he has a strong bodyguard and the place is supposedly under strict police control. The same thing happened with the Unión Patriótica leaders José Antequera and Bernardo Jaramillo. On each occasion, the attackers are arrested or shot on the spot. There is talk of who might be the brains behind the shootings, about 'dark forces', but the investigations never get any further than the men who pull the trigger.

Pizarro's killing gave us a clear picture of what became know as the 'suicide killer'. Leaving aside any speculation as to whether the killers are unaware of what they are getting themselves into — which seems unlikely as novices are not going to be chosen for this kind of thing — we are faced with a surprising phenomenon: young people who are willing to die in action, like Shi'ite terrorists or Japanese kamikaze pilots. With one big difference, namely that these suicide killers are not motivated by any obvious political, ideological or religious motive.

And they are not merely ready to die in spectacular actions like these. Death is a constant presence in their daily existence. Whenever a young man becomes part of the system of contract killings, he knows he will not live long. Many of these youngsters make sure they give instructions about their burial well beforehand. They seem in fact to fear prison more than death.

The aim of the first generation of hired killers was plain: to make money 'to have a good time, live life to the full, and to help the family'. Although their actions were often suicidal because of the risks involved and their spectacular nature, they still had a chance of surviving. Their activities recall those miners in olden days who tied a stone round their necks before diving into rivers to search for a nugget of gold, running the constant risk of their lungs bursting. But in the light of the most recent killings carried out by these youngsters, the question inevitably arises: what does someone need money for, if they know for sure they are going to die, to 'lose the year', as they say in their own language?

Whatever the answer, what is happening with these youngsters, most of them from poor families in Medellín, is a natural consequence of a process that began over a decade ago. It is a revolt by the young people of the poor neighbourhoods, who have discovered in violence, killing for money, and the drug trade, the only possibility of fulfilling their wishes and playing an active part in a society which has closed its doors to them. The suicide killers, if they can be so called, are not some strange exotic phenomenon. They are the direct result of modern Medellín's society and culture.

Medellín is a city at war. The rising death statistics prove it. A disproportionate level of violence afflicts its streets day and night. The crimes which receive most publicity are those related to political violence or the war between the drug cartels. But although these crimes have significant social and political repercussions, statistically they are far less important than everyday acts of violence.

Most of those killed are young men. According to a report by the Medellín local authority, presented at a meeting of the city council, the average age of the victims of violence has fallen dramatically in recent years:

> In 1986 the average age of those killed was between 35 and 45; in 1987 this dropped to between 25 and 35; in 1988 this had fallen to between 20 and 25, and so far in 1989, some 70 per cent of all those who have met violent deaths in the city of Medellín are aged between 14 and 20 years.[6]

The most noteworthy social and cultural aspect of this situation are the adolescent gangs. The campaign mounted by the IVth Brigade in the Aburrá Valley gives us some idea

6. Piedrahita, dCarlos Alberto. Report by the interior ministry to Medellín City Council, session 48, 10 August 1989.

of the scope of the phenomenon. Military intelligence identified no fewer than 120 gangs of contract killers, most of them located in the north-eastern part of the city. According to their calculations, about 3,000 young people were involved. The actual total is probably much higher, but even so, this figure is striking. The gangs were to be found above all in poor areas, and the average age of their members was 16.[7]

One readily observable fact: the map of these gangs in Medellín coincides with the map of the poorest neighbourhoods of the city. In the north-eastern district, the eye of the hurricane, the average monthly earnings per family in 1990 were approximately 47,000 pesos for neighbourhoods such as Santo Domingo, Granizal, Popular, 59,000 for Aranjuez and parts of Manrique, and 82,000 pesos for Campo Valdes.[8]

Earnings in Medellín are inversely proportional to the height of the neighbourhood. The higher one goes, the more overcrowding there is, the poorer the housing, the more inadequate the social services. The neighbourhoods near the tops of the hillsides are those where the presence of armed gangs of youths is most noticeable. This poor area has a population density of 450 inhabitants per hectare, and is almost totally lacking in leisure areas. 'Sixty per cent of the population lives in conditions of abject misery and absolute poverty, which still does not protect it from a consumer society that constantly bombards it with ever greater offers, thereby debasing the ideal of a modern society into a tragic contributory factor of the violence. The image of the juvenile criminal is the clearest expression of this.' The gap between this pressure to consume and available income is present in every city not only in Colombia but in all of Latin America. But many youths in Medellín have found a way to satisfy their desires and in so doing have become a model for all the

7. IVth dBrigade Press Release, 6 March 1990.
8. Mejía, Luz Mercedes, 'The City is Hungry', *El Colombiano*, 23 March 1990 p5c.

others, desperate to achieve the same goal even if they have to pay a high price. Even if they have to pay with their lives.

The popular sectors of society see the state as something distant or hostile. 'The law's here,' they say when the police arrive. The police provide the most constant and the worst image they have of government. They have no confidence in the role of the state as regulator. If before in many areas people took justice into their own hands, now they have all the more reason to do so. They are not afraid of being arrested and tried. Even though the jails are overcrowded, over 95 per cent of crimes go unpunished.

And beyond impunity there is the question of complicity. The IVth Brigade has repeatedly denounced the existence of para-police groups linked to gangs of contract killers.[9] In the testimonies of people from these neighbourhoods and of gang members themselves there are frequent references to the complicity of members of the security forces and the police. This became apparent for example during the assassination attempt on the Unión Patriótica councillor, Gonzalo Alvarez Henao. Ten people were arrested minutes before the attack was due to take place. They were all policemen on active duty.

The reply given by a young gang member when asked what he wanted to do in the future is very revealing, irrespective of how truthful it may be: 'I want to be part of the government, they kill as well, but with the law on their side'. The film-maker Víctor Gaviria is right when he says that the only law that holds true up on the hillsides of Medellín is the law of gravity.[10]

The absence of the state has accentuated the illegal mentality of broad sectors of the population. In May 1982 the largest mass murder then known took place in Medellín. Seven prisoners from Bellavista were killed by a group of hooded men. The policemen guarding their prison van were

9. Information about the case of the Department of Security and Control in Envigado was widely published in the newspapers on 17 March 1990.
10. Restrepo, Laura, 'Our culture of death'. *Semana* magazine, No.408, 27 February-6 March 1990.

disarmed and tied up. Responsibility for the attack was claimed by a group calling itself 'Love for Medellín', a group that became infamous in the years that followed because of its 'clean-up' operations — 'day trips' that ended in death, and the street corner shootings which became daily occurrences in our city. Everyone seemed convinced they had the right to 'cleanse' the neighbourhood or the city of 'undesirable' elements. The authorities and 'respectable' social groups sheltered behind the excuse that the killings were all due to vendettas carried out by the drugs mafia to enforce its 'law'.

It is common practice to reduce the phenomenon of these gangs to the drug trafficking problem. But although the drug cartels have played a fundamental role in their creation and growth, they are not the only ones responsible. The gangs are also linked to other traffickers in death, who do not directly depend on the cartels. A variety of political and social groups also use their services. Even individual citizens have been known to turn to them to solve their problems. The presence of the guerrillas, especially during the peace process of 1985, also led to the creation of some gangs. The guerrilla 'Peace Camps' gave military training to many youths who later formed criminal groups. Former members of the guerrilla groups themselves have turned to various forms of crime, including contract killing.

The formation of the big drug cartels in Medellín from 1975 onwards coincided with the worst industrial and economic recession ever known in Antioquia. Drug trafficking became the only real choice for many sectors of the population, who discovered in it an alternative means of social and economic advancement. Subsequently, the drugs mafia became a role model for the youth of the city, who saw it as a way to fulfil their wishes for status and a lifestyle denied them by the traditional options of study and work. The youthful gangs which are common to any big city were therefore sponsored, or influenced in Medellín by the drug cartels, and this gave them a special meaning.

The influence of the drugs mafia is felt in two ways: firstly, in the large numbers of jobs directly created, including 'couriers' and hired killers; and second, in their extensive social and cultural influence, which has helped create new habits and practices.

## Kamikaze Culture

How are we to explain the fact that a sixteen-year-old youth, from an apparently normal family, assassinates a political leader, a 'boss', knowing full well that he has little chance of surviving or escaping with his freedom?

This question could be asked of many of the new generation, known in the language of the drug traffickers as 'disposable', the kamikaze pilots of those who deal in death. What drives them to commit actions in which they are sure to die?

The usual explanations are not enough. We need first of all to broaden the question. Are these young people the expression of a new culture, a culture of death? Is this a break with or a continuation of the cultural tradition of the Antioquia region? Why do we talk of the loss of our values, as if we had a glorious past to uphold? What other factors influence the logic of these young people, their way of living and dying?

My hypothesis is that a kind of cultural intermixing has taken place that has given rise to the phenomenon of contract killing. The emergence of the gangs is based on three main influences: the social traditions of Antioquia, the culture of low life, and the impact of modernisation. A fourth strand might be punk, which has left its mark in the poor neighbourhoods and is indirectly related to the contract killings.

I would like to make a bold suggestion: that the culture of the Antioquia region is one based on colonisation, on settlement. That is what defines it, gives it its strength and rationale. A world based on settlement. A value system built on the idea of cultivating new land, making money, making a profit. 'That is the basic strength of the people of Antioquia, without which their history cannot be explained'.[11] As the street wall slogan says: *Paisa no muerde paisa* (People from Antioquia don't bite each other)... so who do they 'bite'? And what do they do when there is no-one to 'bite'?

This deep-seated and lively culture is not a solid urban one based on coexistence or shared identity as part of a city. Medellín is an urban conglomerate that has never gelled into a city.

'It is a torn patchwork of village cultures'. The ruling classes in Antioquia were never able to meet the challenge of building the city as a place for meeting and communicating with others, of building a culture of coexistence with a modern ideal. This challenge implied above all the reformulation of an ethical and social ideal to replace the one which led to the founding and settlement of the city in the last century, and which reached a crisis in the 1940s.[12]

The elite contented itself with creating new economic outlets, saw the city as simply a problem of infrastructure and was happy to bask in the memory of a 'great Antioquia' and of 'Antioquia the driving force'. The same vocabulary, only slightly adapted, greets today's conflicts. And now, as then, although the society of Antioquia is bleeding to death, its economy 'is doing fine'.

Everything in Medellín aims to separate, not to integrate. That is the logic of a culture dedicated to profit such as the one now held up as a model. And the result is a split and scattered city. There is not one Medellín but many: cities in the north and south, cities in the valley and up on the hillsides.

In Colombia there are dual systems of education and personal ethical development. The formal one includes

11. Villa, Victor. 'The culture of violence.' In the University of Medellín magazine.
12. 'Rediscovering our values', Medellín City Council, *El Colombiano*, 9 October 1989, p.11A.

school, church, catechism and civic education. Ethical norms, proper behaviour, love of one's neighbour. The other, which apparently is far more effective, is that of daily life. Here, actions that go against the Christian catechism are both possible and accepted.

For the people of Antioquia this dual world is striking. The formal ethical code is one thing; that taught by life is quite different. What matters there is cunning, boldness, to be sharp, to be awake to possibilities: 'The clever live off the fools'... if the main aim is to make money, then it does not matter if in doing so you are going against an ethical or religious norm. Antioquia has traditionally been a region of smugglers. Some of the established aristocratic families made their fortunes in illegal activities that failed to scandalise local society. And sectors of the elite in Antioquia and the rest of Colombia tolerated the drugs mafia for years. Many traditional groups benefitted directly or indirectly from the cocaine boom. They complained that the drug bosses were flashy, common *parvenus*, but they respected their wealth. For years now the Colombian state has accepted narco-dollars through the back door of the Central Bank. Such attitudes perfectly fit the traditional joke: 'Son, make money honestly, but if you can't, make it anyway'.

This dual world can also be seen in the religious sphere. God's pardon for killing is something that has been assumed throughout the long tradition of violence in Colombia. The Church itself has taught it. A rich businessman prays to the Virgin that a deal in which he will be cheating a neighbour goes well for him. And in the neighbourhoods they pray that a stabbing or a shooting will be successful. It is the culture of the rosary and the machete, which nowadays have become the religious medallion and the mini-Uzi.

There are three elements of Antioquia's traditions which are deeply rooted in the adolescent gangs: the desire for money, a religious sentiment, and the law of vengeance. That is why they say: 'money is life'; ' I'll do anything for money'; 'it doesn't matter who the target is, I'm nobody's follower, so long as the dough's right, I'll take on anyone'. And they make a vow to the Virgin of Succour if the job succeeds, that is, 'if the dummy lifts off from earth'.

Religious sentiment survives with extraordinary vigour. But in this religion God the Father has been dethroned. The Virgin Mary has knocked him off his pedestal. 'We pray to the old Man and to the Virgin, but mostly to the Virgin because she is the Mother of God, and a mother is a mother, here and everywhere else'.

The combination Virgin-Mother, which is the golden rule for the hired killers, is synonymous with faithfulness, and unconditional love which does not ask to be requited. The prisoners of Bellavista pray to the Virgin of Succour, saying: 'Remember Holy Virgin Mary that it has never been known for you to refuse help to anyone who turned to you for your protection and succour...'

The youngsters' songs to their mothers repeat the same message:

I'm writing to you from jail
dear mother of my heart
without you I can find no rest
in this dark shadow I live in...

A priest from northeast Medellín, tired of giving absolution to contract killers, reflected on the kind of God these youngsters believe in and concluded: 'They worship a female God, who is tolerant and permissive; they need to find again the male god, the God who punishes and instils fear'.[13] This tolerant image fits in well with the idea that Paco, a gang member from the same neighbourhood, has of God: 'There are people who have done worse things. I believe God forgives, so you can do whatever you like'. The same message

13. Interview conducted by Silvia Duzan and Laura Restrepo.

can be heard in the refrain of a salsa song popular in the area: 'Go on, kill, God will forgive you'.

If the Virgin Mary is the idol in heaven, the mother is the idol on earth. Everything they do, they do in her name. Families in Antioquia have traditionally been noted for a strong maternal figure. The man is king out on the street, but the mother is queen in the home. In the city, and more especially in the poorer neighbourhoods, the old family unit has broken down. Now many women are heads of households. It could be said, without wishing to make a general rule of it, that a large proportion of the teenage gang members come from homes with absentee fathers. This absence may be either physical, or a lack of their active presence in the family. The development of a child's personality implies the presence of a third person, the father, who establishes the law, who prohibits. If the father figure is absent, the child attempts to take his place, to be the law himself.[14]

The interpretation given by a youngster just starting in a gang is striking: 'A mother is the most sacred thing there is; you only have one mother — your father could be any bastard'. This extreme reliance on the mother could in part at least explain the risk that the contract killers accept when they take on a job, their suicidal attitude: 'If the old woman is OK, I'll die happy'. The most recent dreadful killings prove that this attitude, often heard among the youngsters in the poor neighbourhoods, is not simply a pose but an inexplicable choice of sacrifice for the good of the mother and the family. In Medellín, Mother's Day is the most violent day of all.

The hired killers have absorbed the ephemeral sense of time that is typical of our day and age. Life is in the instant. Neither past nor future exist. This leads to a different sense

14. Jimenez, Rocio. 'Psychoanalysis and Violence', Paper presented to the seminar on violence held by the Medellín non-governmental organisations in September 1989.

of the value of life and death: 'Live life for today, even if you die tomorrow'.

The contract killers take the consumer society to its extreme: they turn life (their own and that of their victims) into a commodity to deal in, into a disposable object. In return, death has become part of everyday life. It has become normal to kill and be killed.

Brand names, fashion, the means to consume, are all-important to the hired killers. They are part of their ability to seem powerful. This is one of the aspects which differentiates them from the punks, a counter-culture which rejects the consumer society. The street gangs illustrate the point when discussing their desire to own a motor bike: 'You see those guys on tremendous bikes with fabulous chicks, and you're walking along like nothing, so you want to be able to ride one too, to have one for yourself'.

Their language is full of visual images: 'live like in the movies'; 'put on a video show for someone', 'fatten someone's eyeballs', 'transmitted live and on the spot', 'take a snapshot of someone'. Their way of dressing is equally eye-catching.

This visual culture comes from the mass media, and in particular from the cinema, which has built up a mythology of war, of spectacular action and super-heroes that many of these youths have adopted as their ideal. War and action films are also used as a means to learn tactics.

This myth of super-heroes and victory also influences their suicidal attitude. Their desire to pull off a job successfully becomes an obsession. 'As long as I get the dummy first, I don't care if I go the same way', one of the youngsters said when being warned of the risks he was running.

Antioquia's social life has traditionally been as lacking in a sense of play and enjoyment of the body as it has been rich verbally. Rhythm or sensual pleasure have never been part of its heritage. This is obvious when one listens to traditional music from the region: nostalgic *bambucos* or ballads, *carrilera* music that talks of treachery, revenge, bitterness. Romantic songs like *La Cuchilla*: 'If you don't love me, I'll slash your face', which are inevitably sung when people go out to get drunk, even if they happen to be respectable executives.

Colombia's Caribbean music, which talks of joy and makes the body move, only reached Medellín via the poor. It used to be heard only in the poorest areas: Guayaquil, Palace and the 'dangerous' neighbourhoods. It was the old-style gangsters who made it popular. Only in the last ten years have the people from Antioquia learnt to appreciate and dance to these happy tunes.

Salsa and rumba music now constitutes part of the philosophy, the bible of the youngsters from Medellín's hillside neighbourhoods. They identify with the music because it talks of living today to the full, and the acceptance of death as something to celebrate. The gang members throw a party when one of them dies, and want the same for themselves. Salsa music clearly shows the attitude they have to life and death:

> Soon my lucky day will be here,
> the hope that at my death
> my luck is sure to change.
> (Willy Colón: 'My Lucky Day').

> You have to be happy in life
> because after death you won't get the chance,
> you have to taste all the pleasures,
> you never know when you'll die.
> Life is short so I live it
> enjoying women and wine
> I aim to be happy in life...

> Don't you shed any tears when I die,
> If cry you must, do it while I'm around,
> So I can see if anyone loves me
> and all those who are just fooling me.

> I've had a thousand loves in my life

I've always enjoyed all the pleasures
I aim to be happy in life...

Live your life, it'll soon be gone forever
Enjoy it, always enjoy it,
I'm not leaving this world
If I can't say it's been fun...
Live your life, it'll soon be gone forever...
(Raphy Leavitt, 'Always Happy')

I'm only waiting for
the day when death
takes me with her
when I know my luck will change.
(Fruko, 'The Prisoner')

Some of the burials of gang leaders have become famous,
with their mixture of sadness and carnival. Like that of Flaco,
whose companions kept his body for four days, drinking
liquor, sniffing and smoking and listening to the music he
loved. They carried his body to all the corners of his
neighbourhood and played salsa music during the funeral
mass. Negro's friends accompanied him to the cemetery with
a *mariachi* band. As the coffin was being lowered into the
grave, they made the band play 'But I am still the king', and
fired shots in the air. Cartón's gang danced all through the
wake, and played 'Always Happy' over and over again. In
part of the city it became customary for a while to sit the body
up in its coffin and have a photograph taken alongside it.
Despite their religious beliefs, some mothers have respected
their sons' wishes for their favourite music to be played at the
wake, and for them not to wear mourning. These customs
should not be seen with the spirit of a tourist looking for the
exotic, but seem to indicate a new way of facing death, one
that contrasts sharply with our cultural tradition.

The language of the gang members clearly shows this
acceptance of death. 'We weren't born to breed'; 'we were

born to die'; 'my bags are packed', 'we're playing extra time'. When they go out to do a job, the risk is shrugged off with 'at the most, I'll lose the year'. To their dead friends they say 'man, you're doing your thing'.

It is curious to note that three words from the Antioquia tradition are the ones most often used to describe a dead body. *El traido* (the brought one) is the name given to the present which the infant Jesus brings to children on Christmas Eve, but is also used of the intended victim of a contract killing. *El muñeco* (the dummy) used to be made of rags and gunpowder on New Year's Eve, but now has come to mean the dead person. *El paseo* (the day trip) refers to the old habit that many Medellín families had of leaving the city at the weekend to find somewhere in the countryside to spend the day and cook a stew for all to share. Now it means being taken out along those same roads to be killed: the roadsides have been used for a number of years as a dump for dead bodies.

This celebration of death is an extension of the low-life values praised in the traditional popular music of the poor neighbourhoods, such as the tango. A man, a real man, will never back down, will never betray his friends, lives and dies according to his own laws: all this has become part of the tradition of today's contract killer. But it is above all salsa music that defines the attitudes of these city youths. Salsa tells them of Pedro Navaja, of Juanito Alimaña, of tough guys and their neighbourhoods. This has made it a key element in the young gang members' social and cultural identity.

## Gang Society

Although there have been middle-class teenage gangs, the vast majority of them come from the poorer areas of the city. In many neighbourhoods they have become the main socialising factor for children and youths. The young are drawn to a gang not just for economic reasons but because it offers them a social role that gives them identity and cohesion.

The gangs provide rituals, power struggles, a sense of territory — such things represent a demand for social recognition, telling people 'we exist, we are, we can'.

Adolescent gangs differ from the professional criminal fraternity in that the latter seeks to be anonymous and hidden. For the gang members, money and weapons are there to be shown off. You're not a 'real man' to go unnoticed: you are there to be openly feared or admired. This underlying strand of personal and collective identity underpins the groups' cohesive power.

In many gangs, the formation process is spontaneous. A group of kids in a neighbourhood who get together because they are friends and neighbours is transformed, sometimes slowly, sometimes remarkably quickly, into a proper gang. Some of the gang members start with petty crime, mugging people or holding up stores with fake weapons; bit by bit their weapons improve, they can buy motor bikes, and their operational capacity increases. Gang leadership is a decisive factor: the gang usually adopts the name of the person who has become the reference point for the group.

Conflict with the authorities, with the local population and with other gangs then serves to unite the group much more closely and leads to a complex system of relationships. A clear demarcation of gang territory is essential not only to exercise power but for the purposes of defence.

Relations with the community are different in every case. They are helped when the gang acquires good connections and takes on large-scale operations. Then the gangs help with security in the neighbourhoods, they get rid of petty criminals, and sometimes help people out with money. In this way they gain influence and sympathy.

This positive image can be spoilt if they abuse their power. Usually, however, they succeed in keeping the support of most of the people and so convert their neighbourhoods into a rearguard where they can operate with a degree of safety.

But if a gang is unsuccessful in doing 'deals' that bring in big criminal jobs, they can turn against their own neighbourhood. They soon become dismissed as 'small fry' or 'runts'. These groups are usually made up of very young boys and are extremely violent towards their own neighbours. They kill almost without thinking, and sometimes commit sexual offences.

When they take on their own community in this way, they make themselves vulnerable. Sooner or later, people react, either by forming their own self-defence groups, or by collaborating with the authorities.

The internal structure of the gangs depends on how specialised the group is. They usually combine a personal, vertical line of command with ideas of loyalty and friendship. They apply codes and norms of behaviour strictly. Yet their propensity to show off and to boast of their achievements is another weak spot. All the members of a gang are known in their own neighbourhoods.

Specialist gangs often go beyond the confines of one particular neighbourhood, and are organised in many different ways. They may be small groups which engage in increasingly serious and professional crime, or individuals brought together by one leader from different parts of the city.

These gangs work for themselves or on behalf of someone else. When they get power and money they can also offer their own services. This leads to the setting-up of so-called 'offices', run by groups that have great operational capacity.

To a large extent, these specialist gangs are made up of survivors. Very few of the youngsters manage to reach this stage. 'Perhaps with the years and with the possibility of living more fully they will settle down, they will become real adults,' as one of their defence lawyers puts it.

## Imagining the Future

The gangs will never be controlled as long as they represent practically the only model of socialisation and identification offered the new generations in the poor neighbourhoods of

Medellín. As long as children grow up facing violence every day, and see death as the centre of the world of their imagination.

In the schools of these neighbourhoods, today's young pupils write stories in which all the charm of the past has vanished. Now they see themselves as the heroes of stories full of death, or in which 'evil' men impose their ways. This for example is how one such child sees his own neighbourhood:

'The gang on motor bikes lived in the village and didn't let anyone sleep. They made a lot of noise but nobody said anything because they were very bad men. Since this motor-bike gang came to the village everybody was leaving it until one day the village was empty and the gang stayed there forever.'

A twelve-year-old boy in his first year at secondary school gave the following reply when asked what he wanted to be:

'I'd like to be a killer but I want me and my family to be respected. Just like Ratón, who has been shot now, but who was a guy who said nothing but killed anyone that stepped out of line. He would stand there with his 9mm pistol and if anyone stared at him he'd say: What are you staring at? And if they got cheeky he'd kill them, spit on them and walk off laughing. That's how I'd like to be'.

Many of these children and youths will become the new 'Desquites' of Gonzalo Arango's prophecy. Colombia has not yet been able to meet the challenge of creating a worthy life for its new generations.

We are in a dance of life and death. Like tribal peoples, we continue to offer the gods human sacrifices. Unlike them, we expect no reward. The contract killers are our society writ large: 'we'll do anything to get our hands on money'. They are simply the open sore, the external symptoms of an illness which afflicts the whole body of society. Their actions pose essential questions about the coherence of the ethical and social basis of our society. Unfortunately, they only become of interest when they strike at the nerve centres of power. If their violence is simply directed at each other, if it can be dismissed as a war within the poor neighbourhoods, then the state and most sectors of society remain unconcerned.

Ten years after the alert was sounded over contract killings and adolescent gangs, the state has still not come up with any comprehensive stategy to combat the problem. This not only demonstrates the power of the violence, but our own powerlessness: Colombian society is paralysed, and has been unable to develop any successful ideas to prevent it spreading.

The culture of the Antioquia region has many strong, positive elements. It is a vital, lively, and deeply-rooted tradition that is as capable of promoting life as it is of bringing death. What seems to have happened is that in these troubled times its negative side has come to the fore, whereas its positive aspects have become dispersed in a sea of despondency.

This glance at the cultural aspects of the gang phenomenon is of course very partial and limited. It is also hazardous if it is not taken as an invitation to extend our knowledge in a clear-sighted way that avoids stereotypes. The hired killer has become part of our social and cultural make-up. They are one side of the problem. The other is made up of the 'businessmen' and 'clients' who use the killers' services, and who are not limited to drug traffickers. Many sectors of our society, political and others, are hidden behind the smokescreen created by these adolescent killers.

The possible ways out of this situation are closely linked to the solution of the major problems that Colombia is now facing, to the proposed reforms of the state, and in particular of its system of justice. But they call first and foremost for the creation of schemes in the poor neighbourhoods that will offer real alternatives to the children and young people who want to play an active role in society, who want some choice in their lives. If we cannot do this, all that will happen will be more crocodile tears, shed whenever Colombia is shaken by yet another inevitable spate of killings.

# Books from the Latin America Bureau

Brazil: War on Children
Gilberto Dimenstein
Introduction by Jan Rocha

In *Brazil: War on Children*, journalist Gilberto Dimenstein interweaves first hand reportage, interviews and statistics to paint a picture of life for the children. He discovers a world of pimps, muggers, prostitutes and petty criminals; homeless children who live in fear of sudden death at the hands of the off-duty police and other vigilantes who make up Brazil's death squads.

The author interviews the Church workers who risk becoming death squad targets by befriending the children and trying to bring them hope. He talks to the authorities who turn a blind eye, to the killers and to the children themselves.

An introduction by Jan Rocha, *The Guardian*'s Brazil correspondent, shows how the children are just the most visible casualties of one of the most unequal societies on earth.

'It should be the duty of everyone who cares about children in any respect to read this book.'
Brian Milne, *International Children's Rights Monitor*

Gilberto Dimenstein is a leading young Brazilian journalist, winner of the 1991 Marie Moors Cabot Prize, awarded by the Columbia School of Journalism for an outstanding international journalist.

1991 £5.75/US$11.50 96 pages ISBN 0 906156 62 9

### Colombia: Inside the Labyrinth
Jenny Pearce

Colombia is officially a Latin American success story, with steady growth and political stability. Yet it has become notorious through the activities of the Medellín and Cali cartels and the violence surrounding the cocaine trade.

*Colombia: Inside the Labyrinth* unravels the threads of this paradoxical country. Exploring the economic and social forces which condemn a quarter of the population to absolute poverty, it examines the role of the political parties, trade unions, guerrillas and civic movements in Colombia today.

'Pearce covers an amazing breadth of events, bringing together a mass of up-to-date facts and opinions in this indispensable reference book.'
Amnesty

Jenny Pearce is lecturer in Third World politics at the University of Bradford and the author of *Under the Eagle: US Intervention in Central America and the Caribbean* (LAB, 1982) and *Promised Land: Peasant Rebellion in Chalatenango, El Salvador* (LAB, 1986).

1990 £9.00/US$19.50 312 pages ISBN 0 906156 44 0

## Faces of Latin America
Duncan Green

Exploring the region from Argentina to Venezuela, *Faces of Latin America* describes the people and the processes which have shaped modern Latin America.

The book celebrates the vibrant culture of Latin America's peoples and looks at some of the key actors in the region's turbulent politics with chapters on the military, democracy, the guerrillas, indigenous peoples, the Church and the women's movement.

*Faces of Latin America* also traces the roots of the continent's most pressing issues — underdevelopment and poverty, the environmental crisis, and the fight for democracy.

'A wonderful introduction. Duncan Green has humanized our neighbours without sentimentalizing them. Clearly the work of an author who knows Latin America — and cares.'
Richard Fagen, Stanford University

'Lucid, readable, realistic and up-to-date.'
Hugh O'Shaughnessy, *The Observer*

Duncan Green is a researcher at the Latin America Bureau and author of *Nicaraguans Talking* (LAB, 1989).

1991 £10.00/US$17.50 224 pages ISBN 0 906156 59 9

The above prices are for paperback editions and include post and packing. Write for a complete list of LAB books to Latin America Bureau, 1 Amwell Street, London EC1R 1UL.

LAB books are distributed in North America by Monthly Review Press, 122 West 127 Street, New York, NY 10001.

The Latin America Bureau is a small, independent, non-profit-making research organisation established in 1977. LAB is concerned with human rights and related social, political and economic issues in Central and South America and the Caribbean. We carry out research, publish books, and establish support links with Latin American groups. We also brief the media, run a small documentation centre and produce materials for teachers.